HEALING THE WOUNDED HEART

Healing the Wounded Heart

Limiting the damage of
childhood bereavement

Pat Wynnejones

Hodder & Stoughton

LONDON SYDNEY AUCKLAND

British Library Cataloguing in Publication Data
A record for this book is available from the British Library

ISBN 0 340 67888 7

Typeset by Hewer Text Composition Services, Edinburgh
Printed and bound in Great Britain by
Caledonian International Book Manufacturing Ltd, Glasgow

Hodder and Stoughton Ltd
A Division of Hodder Headline PLC
338 Euston Road
London NW1 3BH

To John

Contents

Acknowledgements

I would like to thank all those who in their various ways have contributed to this book; who have been generous with their time, their wisdom and their willingness to share their sorrows and memories of painful experience.

Some have been directly involved with major disasters, and some have opened up their personal tragedies in conversations and letters, most of which are from people who have been willing to look back thirty years or so and speak of their childhood hurts. They have given a valuable retrospective angle on our understanding of childhood bereavement.

Others have given me insight into special areas of care. Mrs Anne Lingley of Quidenham Children's Hospice kindly invited me to see their work for terminally ill children and their families; in an extended interview Detective Inspector Mick Mann gave me a comprehensive account of the principles and practice of policing in a changing role; and I am also grateful to Christine Hawkins for the case histories in Chapter 3 and her account of the often overlooked role of the health visitor; to May Moore for her account of her work with parentless children in a refugee camp in Cyprus; to Peter Zimmerman and the Prison Fellowship; to the Rev. David Kingdon for permission to use his story; and to the Rev. Dr David Hartenberger of Albuquerque and the Rev. Cyril Dann of Hobart for supplying useful sources of help for American and Australian readers.

At a practical level, the librarians in the National Youth Agency have patiently found material that I needed; and I am very grateful to Robert Haggar for his perseverance in preparing the manuscript for the publishers.

I have greatly valued the encouragement of my family. Lastly, I wish to thank my brother for many hours of helpful discussion on the text.

1

'When I was a child': how children learn about death

When grief goes wrong

My mother died when I was five and a half: she apparently had not had good health since my birth and eventually died in hospital of kidney failure. My dad died in hospital of throat cancer when I was seven.

No one put it into words to me that my parents had died. I gathered everything from overheard conversations of adults and the over-riding factor of the ensuing years was that no one talked about my mum and dad to me. My sister and I never verbally acknowledged to each other that our parents were dead, nor how we felt. We grew up bonded in our sorrow but in little else. In turn I found it impossible to tell anyone that my parents were dead. I believe this lack of communication helped to make me unable to demonstrate love to others and I developed a cynical outlook on life in my teens and twenties.

Our widowed grandmother provided a home for us, although she was in her sixties and her health was beginning to suffer. She provided food and clothing and shelter, but I have no recollection of receiving affectionate words or embraces.

I lived a fairly solitary life as a child, unable to express love yet longing to be loved. What I did express was anger, perhaps cloaking fear. I frequently threw temper tantrums and was insolent to my grandmother. I can vividly remember saying, 'I hate you!' on many occasions. I just wanted someone to wrap their arms round me when I cried and tell me everything would be all right. I needed someone big enough to contain all my turbulent emotions. I carried misery around inside me which seemed to prevent me letting myself go.[1]

It was not till forty years later that Margery finally grieved for her parents and for the little girl she had been when she lost them. Hers is by no means an exceptional story.

In her experience we can see some of the reasons why grief can 'go wrong'. Buried hurts have a way of insisting that eventually they be heard. The mind may put up 'memory blocks' to protect itself against pain, but some chance happening, sight or sound may demolish the blocks, and the sudden release of memory may produce a totally unpredictable outcome. There was, for example, the occasion when an airline pilot with his VC10 full of passengers was seized by panic when approaching Heathrow. Paralysed with fear he was unable to land – the legacy of unresolved grief for the mother he lost when he was a small boy.

Children may appear curiously detached and unmoved at the time and then, like adults who show little emotion, meet trouble later. It is only since a generation of closely watched bereaved children have grown up that it has been possible to consider the long-term effects of losing a parent in childhood, and the difference that can be made by effective help at the time. Before that it was a neglected area, dismissed in ignorance with 'children bounce back'. Some may do – many do not.

Spotlight on sorrow

Large-scale tragedies from all over the world (for example, the sinking of the ferry *Herald of Free Enterprise*, the bombing in Oklahoma and the massacres in Tasmania) have focused a spotlight on the plight of children who are suddenly plunged into the totally destabilising experience of a parent's death; and there is now great public interest, media coverage and a desire to understand. And rightly so, for this is a matter which concerns not only the well-being of the individual child, but the future of society; for today's children are tomorrow's parents, and depression, often one of the spin-offs of childhood bereavement, is one of the commonest psychiatric disorders. It can disrupt family life and cause severe social problems.

The outcome depends to a large extent on the care given at the time and the child's age. Children like Margery who lose a parent, especially a mother, in their early years are very vulnerable. Those who meet such a tragedy before the age of three or four, while they have no real understanding of death and its finality, are more likely to suffer personality problems in adult life, such as low self-esteem and difficulty in making relationships. These effects can throw a shadow over their whole future, especially if, like Margery, they are unable to share their anxiety and sorrow, or to ask questions that would satisfy their growing conceptual awareness.

It is important to understand how the concept of death develops, for without a grasp of the physical finality of death children are not able to grieve. If we know what children understand, and at what age, we shall be better able to talk with them at an appropriate level and to help those who have suffered a loss. Otherwise attempts to explain the situation to a small child may only make it more confusing.

Close and real

In previous centuries this problem would not have existed. There would have been a general assumption that children knew what death entailed because it was all around them. High infant mortality, diseases born of ignorance and poverty, and lack of institutionalised ageing meant that grandparents, parents and even siblings would die within sight or touch. If they did not encounter loss in their actual experience they would meet it in their stories. Death is a frequent theme in nineteenth-century children's stories such as *Little Women*, *The Water Babies* and George Macdonald's fairy tales.

We should realise that, far from being morbid, this attitude was actually far more psychologically healthy than the subsequent trend when the subject was excluded from children's stories and became taboo. Since then, one result of medical advance has been the assumption that no one ought to die, and we have made a problem for ourselves as death has become thought of as failure and its remoteness has added to its terror. 'The dominant culture wishes to pretend that the dark side of life does not exist,' as Dr Bruno Bettelheim, the psychoanalyst and writer on the child's subconscious mind, has said, 'but real life is not all sunny.'

Death comes with other anxieties into the child's inner consciousness, but fears can be dealt with when they are spoken of openly, not in hushed voices as unmentionable secrets. It is the adults whose fear and reticence communicate their own anxieties to children. In the past the subject could not be avoided because there were few families who did not lose a member at an early age. The idea of 'death education' would have been a nonsense to children who had seen a sibling die in the next cot. Today's children do not have this 'advantage'. Where do they gather their ideas from?

Frameworks for learning

The home background

The most influential source will be the home, for a child's understanding of death, as of life, develops through observations and ideas gathered in the course of his or her daily life. Gradually children takes on board aspects of the subject, like pieces of a jigsaw puzzle: and these will include opinions about what may follow death, in particular the beliefs of their own family. Children from different backgrounds and cultures will gather different impressions as to what is involved in saying that a person is dead. They will be influenced by the attitudes of the people round them – the way they talk about death and behave when someone dies. Do they weep, perhaps scream, or keep a 'stiff upper lip'? Is there whispering, evasion and mystery? Are clichés used, such as 'fallen asleep', 'lost' or 'passed over', which can leave a child mystified and fearful?

On the other hand it may well be helpful if the accepted thinking of the family includes the idea that a loved one lives on in another dimension. As one child wrote, 'It is the thought that someone you love has been extinguished that is truly unbearable.' Most religions represented in this country would accept that death is not the end of our identity.

Rhythms of life: the world around us

For a child living in the country death may be a more familiar affair than for the town child. Death is no stranger on the farm. It is part of the order of things. The constant process of seasonal change and renewal must make a deep, though maybe not conscious, impression. Country children have the advantage of seeing life in an ordered setting and even of perceiving it as beautiful in the bare patterns of trees and pure whiteness of winter landscapes.

Similarly, children who grow up within the framework of a religion have the advantage of seeing life in an ordered setting. The sense of continuity inherent in the rituals for coming into life and going out of it, in the accepted beliefs and certainties, imparts a feeling of security. Ritual answers a basic need in children, and festivals, as for example those of the church year, give a powerful visual aid of death as part of a continuum of the whole of human existence.

Just pretending? The impact of the media

On the other hand, most of today's children will have their ideas shaped by what they see on television, which will include news coverage of battle scenes, frozen corpses and starving children. They may well see several dramatised murders in the course of an evening, including close-ups of someone being strangled, knifed or kicked to death. They may even watch violent videos and the late-night horror film with its corpses, ghosts and excursions into the occult. The Report of the Parliamentary Group Video Enquiry revealed that a surprisingly high proportion of children over the age of seven had watched 'video nasties' and would therefore have their idea of death associated with horror, sadism and fear.

We may not always realise what the long-term effect may be when children are exposed only to gruesome images of death. Birth is of course invariably portrayed as beautiful and joyful, while death is shown as overwhelmingly bitter. But there are other aspects that should not be forgotten, such as heroism and sacrifice, and it is right that children should know that there are some things that people have thought worth dying for.

People sometimes ask whether children's perceptions of death are confused by the make-believe of cartoons. The conversation of five- and six-year-olds in the infant school showed no such confusion:

Question: Do you know Tom and Jerry?
Andrew (5): Yes, they're a cartoon. And sometimes they're sort of pretending to be dead.
Alison (6): Sometimes in films people die because there's a sword stuck in them, but they're really not dead. They're probably plastic toys.
Andrew (5): They're sort of acting, but really somebody makes the film, so nobody's really dead.

These children are clear about the real world and the celluloid one. However, we should bear in mind that even at this age they may not grasp the personal application as an older child would.

School, seeds and stories

Infant schools offer a wide variety of situations for learning about biological aspects of death, such as growing seeds, collecting conkers, studying the life cycles of creatures. Spiritual aspects may be explored through stories such as *The Snow Queen* and *The Happy Prince*, which offer different perspectives on death and address children's anxieties below the level of conscious thought with the assurance that love is eternal.

Although there may be some formal teaching about death in the primary school, it is generally accepted that children learn most effectively from personal experience. As we might expect, a study of four- and five-year-olds in Northern Ireland confirmed that those who have lived close to death have a more advanced understanding than those for whom it is remote. This will apply not only as far as relatives and friends are concerned, but even for those who have lost a dearly loved pet, which is for many children their first experience of grief. The occasion should not be trivialised with insensitive remarks such as 'We'll get you another puppy'. We do not know how deep the emotional investment may be:

'Dear little fish. I wish you did not have to die. But I will love you for ever and ever,' wrote a six-year-old.

The varied ideas and imagery that children gather in connection with death colour, and eventually complete, their picture, possibly playing some part in their response to bereavement. Although we cannot foresee what awaits our children in this unpredictable world, we can make a positive contribution to their future by encouraging the formation of a healthy mental picture, controlling television viewing, excluding the violent and horrific, and talking about death as the subject arises in a natural uninhibited way, as a process that completes life, not as an end but as a transition.

Completing the jigsaw

Realisation

> 'If I could, I would make you alive again,' said Pippi. It was a
> baby bird that was dead. It had fallen from the nest and been
> killed. (Astrid Lindgren, *Pippi Longstocking*, 1950.)

The concept of death does not arrive complete: it grows
gradually along with other concepts and understanding of life.
An adult perception is built up by the accumulation of compo-
nents which our children grasp at different stages. From their
earliest years they can hardly escape noticing that living things
do not last for ever. By the age of four Robin and Adam were
able to explain their criteria for knowing dead from live leaves:

> Robin (4.3): These leaves are crumpled up. Those are
> straight.
> Adam (4.8): These leaves have died. Those have not died.
> Alive is when they stay a long time.

However, children of this age may still be unclear about the
nature of life, and attribute it to inanimate things. A group of
four- to six-year-olds produced the following thoughts:

> Sunshine is alive because it is very hot, and glasses are alive
> because they are helping someone to see, but shoes are dead
> because they only move if someone is wearing them.

Separation

As their understanding grows it is important that children
should have opportunities for asking questions and bringing
any anxieties and fears into the open, so that they do not spin
unspoken fantasies. For children it is not death itself that holds
most terror, but fear of separation. Anxiety about being

separated from their mother develops from the first months of life as a child becomes conscious that he or she has an identity of their own. Separation anxiety reaches its peak about the age of two and becomes an integral part of the death concept.

The sadness of this separation is deeply felt. A four-year-old, having drawn a live hedgehog, refused to draw a dead one, 'because it was too sad'. Claire, distressed by the sight of a dead tadpole floating lugubriously in the tank, commented: 'Isn't it sad? It can't be with its friends any more.'

A six-year-old was so alarmed by the thought of having to be parted from his mother by death that he told her that she would have to stay in the coffin with him when he died.

Jon, aged five, climbed into his parents' bed one morning. 'Daddy,' he said, 'one day we will have to part. But then we will be together again for ever.'

Movement, or lack of it, will be one of the most obvious things a child will observe; the immobility of a dead creature will be one of the earliest aspects of death that he can identify, a piece of the jigsaw that fits easily into place and that makes a useful yardstick.

The finality of death is much more difficult to comprehend, and it is not until the age of about six that children are able to grasp the fact that the parent they have lost will never be returning. However hard it seems, it is better not to leave children in doubt. This harsh truth must be sensitively handled and is perhaps best conveyed pictorially. The life cycle of the dragonfly provides a perfect analogy: it can be seen that once the grub has metamorphosed into a creature of the air it could not exist in the water of the pond. Return is impossible.

The picture of a journey is an alternative.

One day God called Enoch to take him for a walk. They talked and they walked so far that God said to Enoch, 'Enoch, you are very tired, so I think you should come home with me.'

Small children can understand walking and getting tired, and as they mature they can grasp that life is a journey. In a

Christian context the emphasis can be upon where Mummy has gone, not upon the fact that she is not coming back.[2]

Searching questions

Children often have confused ideas about the causes of death, and on hearing of a death may ask, 'Who killed him?' like primitive man assuming that it must be violent. Or they may look for an authoritarian reason and wonder, 'Am I being punished?'

If there is a death in the family the real cause should be explained truthfully and simply and as soon as possible. We cannot tell how much a child may pick up from overheard conversations or know instinctively. *Honesty is the first requirement of healing: but answer questions only as they arise* and do not pre-empt them or go into details for which the child may not be ready.

Many questions may be asked and answered for the purpose of reassurance – that the other parent is not about to die, nor the child herself; that people do not necessarily die when they go into hospital; that there will be someone to look after her. Time should be spent quietly sorting these out.

A Milky Way in heaven

By the age of seven children will be forming a fuller concept of death, but they may not grasp the idea that every bodily function ceases. They may picture people walking about and eating or drinking somewhere under the ground or up in heaven. Ruth, aged five, and David, just four, were delighted to hear that their father would not need his stick up in heaven, and three-year-old Katie tried to comfort her mother: 'Never mind, Mummy, I'm going to take a Milky Way to heaven and share it with Daddy.'

It is natural for children to want to know what may happen to the 'real' person after death and to find thoughts of heaven comforting and right. Such questions must be answered in the light of our own beliefs and with a regard for the child's family and background. We should not be surprised at the ideas children may produce in this respect, nor look for more advanced thinking than we would expect in others. A new life in a different dimension, however it may be described, is a way of expressing what many people believe to be the truth.

Heaven lies about us in our infancy

During the years between seven and ten there is a great leap forward in children's ability to formulate abstract ideas, and their personal writing reveals that by ten they have reached an adult understanding of what death entails. They have a clear idea of biological death:

> Death is when the body stops functioning. All the major cells stop so the body stops too.

They are aware of its universality:

> When death comes people should learn to accept it, because it always comes sooner or later.

Many comment on issues they have probably seen discussed on television, such as reincarnation, euthanasia and the occult. In one group of ten-year-olds, all the writers were interested in what may await them after death, and out of sixty pieces of writing only one expressed a belief that death means extinction. There were many expressions of belief in personal survival and vivid images of what heaven may be like:

> I tried to think what would happen when you die. I thought that you would be taken by angels to a place that was very peaceful and beautiful.

> When you get to the end of the tunnel there is a garden full of roses and daisies and all the flowers you can think of. There are lots of people playing in this wonderful garden and there is no evil anywhere.

The next picture was of my friends Ranjan and Saleem. Then I saw Jesus who said, 'Go into heaven through the everlasting gates and into eternal life.'

These writings show that by the time they are ready to leave the primary school children's minds are open to all the aspects of death that the adult mind can contemplate.

In my beginning is my end

There will be times when we have to admit that we do not know all the answers, and that opinions differ – but this is good for children to know. At this age, too, we can tell them that there are two things that we can do with our grief – either we can let the anger and pain spoil our lives, or we can use our own pain to help heal other wounded hearts. The way each child copes with the idea of death and responds to the loss of someone dear is a very individual thing. There are no universal guidelines, but there are certain factors that do have a bearing, which we will consider in the next chapter.

2

No universal yardstick: factors with a bearing on the child's response to loss

Home base: the importance of security and stable home life

> It was very difficult to get them to contradict each other, even though we children often did our best to drive a wedge between them, as children do, in the hope we could get our own way . . . They pulled together in family discipline, avoided favouritism, and thereby made the home a secure and consistent shelter.[1]

When a child loses a mother or father it is the quality of the home in which he has been reared that gives him the power to survive. This is not something that can be acquired in a matter of days without any effort. It requires a firm relationship of love and trust between the parents, and that means endless patience, tact, making mistakes and forgiving them, starting over again and not giving up. This hard-forged bond is then gradually transmitted to the children.

Firm bedrock

The world is changing in a bewildering way, which makes it all the more important that children should have a stable home,

from which they can learn to view without hassle the changing
scene around them. No matter how society changes, the top
priority for children is what goes on within the walls of the
home, for this is what will give them an inner strength to
support them when they meet the shock of bereavement,
whether it is in childhood or later in life. It is not a matter of
money, social class or status, but of love, trust and holding
together.

It is better to have loved and lost . . .

Devastating though it is to lose either a father or a mother, it is
better to have once had the experience of such a home and to
keep the stored memory. It is harder for children from homes
where there has been conflict and bitterness when one of those
parents dies. Children themselves feel that a father who dies
remains part of their being in a way that a father who has left
them does not.

> My husband died seven years ago as the result of a car
> accident . . . my children were seven and ten years old . . .
> they both now feel it was better their dad died than simply left
> them. We constantly find divorce and separation is a form of
> bereavement which many children go through and needs
> careful handling. Our children are emotionally damaged by
> such situations which are so often ignored.

Having said this, the choice of single parenthood may sometimes be the only possible adjustment to a difficult marital
situation: better, for instance, than leaving a child open to
physical or sexual abuse, where safety and well-being cannot
be guaranteed. Those who find they have to make such a choice
should take courage, for it is still possible with faith and
determination to fashion the kind of home base that will enable
children to grow up strong and independent. Everything still
depends on love, trust and holding together.

A system of belief within the home brings a dimension of

support and comfort different from anything that can be offered by human kindness or the commonplace neighbourly platitudes.

I have said in several places that the phrase 'the peace of God' became all the more real to me . . . I couldn't really say that Nichola and Timmy had a faith that helped them through, but on the other hand they saw the outworking of faith in me and in the church people, not giving way when a weak faith might have cracked.

Faces of calamity: the way death comes

Death may come in different ways, but no matter how it comes, if it is the death of someone close it is always a shock. One way is not necessarily worse than another.

It may be a death that could be naturally foreseen, as, for example, that of an elderly grandparent; it may have been expected, as in a long terminal illness; it may come suddenly out of the blue, as in a heart attack, an accident or a violent death. Or it may be one of those particularly difficult happenings when there is no body to say a farewell to, a drowning or a disappearance where there is no visible death event.

A 'foreseeable death'

Elizabeth wrote a letter suggesting how to explain the death of a grandmother:

Obviously a 'normal' death is easier for both adults and children to accept. Grandmother was old; she had a lovely life; she was very tired. (A special sort of tiredness, otherwise the child will panic every time Mum says, 'Gosh, I'm exhausted.') Her body needs a rest for ever; she is, in some way we can't understand, with Jesus.

However, the fact that death is easier to explain doesn't necessarily make it easier to accept. Jamie had been a tug-of-love child, staying with his mother for a few days, then with his father, while each tried to convince him that he really belonged to one or the other. The elderly grandmother, who stood back from the argument and did not try to convince him of anything but her unchanging support and love, was the only stable element in his life. When she died he went to pieces.

A long and depressing terminal illness

Reactions to terminal illness can be many and varied; much will depend on whether the child has been brought into the situation and knows what is going on, and what to expect, or whether he has been left in the dark.

Two children, aged five and six, who were allowed to be involved in the care of their terminally ill grandmother found it a learning experience:

> I think they are more aware of life having an end and what old age means . . . they were involved in most of her care and we made them as much part of the situation as we could, given their age and understanding. It was a sad, useful and good experience and memory for all of us and the children seem to have gained, not lost, from it.

A long illness gives a child time to experience some of the sorrow and work through some of the grief before the actual event.

Paul was a young successful businessman with three sons – Anthony, aged seven, Andrew, four, and little Jeremy, just three months – when he was diagnosed as having inoperable cancer. He and Jenny decided he should come home from hospital and that they would bring the boys home from a holiday to complete the family. The two older boys were free to come and go and ask questions. Anthony certainly understood what was happening and cried for many nights as he went to sleep. Wisely, Jenny would leave him for a little while before she went in to comfort him. Often they cried together.

Children who live close to a parent who is dying may have to cope with seeing distressing changes in appearance:

> I explained that he still had his lovely face but because he was ill for quite a while it had become thinner and he had lost all of his hair. (He used to wear a cap or woolly hat most of the time.) I got a couple of photos and put them in frames so that we could remember Daddy as he was.

It is also possible that a child may not notice the signs of declining health, so that the death will come with as much of a shock as if it had happened suddenly.

Sudden death – accident, heart attack, violent death

These deaths are likely to produce extreme reactions, from numbness and disbelief to screaming and tears. They are a terrible blow to the whole family, and children will be affected by the way other family members react to the shock:

> My father died about three years ago in a car crash. It happened so suddenly that everyone was in a state of shock. When Mum told me that Daddy was dead, my knees started shaking. I almost fell down. My sister Peg screamed when she found out.[2]

Deaths that are caused by violence, whether the result of war, disaster, murder or massacre – such as those at Dunblane and Hobart – are as traumatic for children as for everyone else. They may suffer from post-traumatic stress disorder, when they continually have recurrent images of what they have seen, in dreams and flashbacks which they cannot get out of their minds. It is similar to the condition of children who have been exposed to the extreme sadism and violence of 'video nasties'.

Violent bereavement may cause adults and children alike to be in a state of shock for a long time. There may be physical effects such as digestive troubles, sleeplessness and nightmares, from which recovery gradually becomes possible as they work through their grief.

No visible death event

The importance of the funeral for children in providing a 'proper' ending and time to say goodbye is commented on more fully in Chapter 5; but there are occasions when a funeral is not possible because there is no body, as in a drowning or a disappearance. It is particularly painful not to be able to mark the loss of someone dear in a dignified manner, with the service and ritual that testify to the worth of the one who is lost.

When Marion's husband was lost at sea the lack of such a meaningful occasion gave her great distress: 'It may seem morbid, but we didn't have a body. There is something "Monday morningish", a new beginning, about a funeral with a body present. The two memorial services we attended did not compensate for this.'

Andrew Sewell, whose daughter 'disappeared' in India, had to wait five years before she was legally regarded as dead. 'This', he wrote, 'is a particularly fraught matter for those who find themselves with no "death event".'

We need to recognise that there are other ways of losing a parent than by death and they may be even more distressing and destructive to a child's well-being. The desertion of a mother or father when a home breaks up means more than the absence of that parent. It carries the implication of rejection: while it is possible to see that no one can help dying, when a parent leaves and makes another home it gives the abandoned child the impression that she is not only not loved but unlovable, not only not valued but worthless. The psychological damage of such pain may be life-long or perhaps only healed at last by marriage and the regenerating love of children.

The damage to a whole family when a parent goes to prison is not generally recognised by society at large, for it comes within the taboo of shameful secrets. Yet the situation cries out for generous human understanding and help. If the imprisonment is for life, the father is permanently lost to the children growing up; if it is a situation where one parent has killed the other, the children lose both and are orphaned at a blow. In any event the families suffer ostracism and shame (see Appendix III).

Children who are caught up in wars and disasters during which they become separated from their parents suffer from the uncertainty of not knowing what has happened to them or whether they will ever see them again. It is a form of loss similar to bereavement but without the finality that only death can give. A child may live for years in a protracted bereavement, during which she steels herself for a worse outcome while hoping against hope for a possible best (see Appendix III).

The person inside: the personality factor

From the time they are born, long before they meet the pressures of society, our children will have inherited personality traits along with their physical attributes which will influence the way they will respond to circumstances and the crises of life, including loss. Some of them will become what we see as natural survivors, which is a way of saying that something buoys them up in trouble and enables them to survive. This 'something' may well include carefully nurtured character traits.

The sense of trust is the cornerstone of personality; it is the first character trait to develop and usually the first casualty of any major loss. It is built on the experience of being loved, and is nurtured by the way in which all the baby's needs, physical and emotional, are met by the mother and father. Unconditional love is vital from babyhood to adolescence, for without it the personality is starved of the ability to give out love in return:

> I grew up in a sort of vacuum with no love demonstrated and consequently being unable to demonstrate love myself.

Without love and trust the growing child does not have the confidence to branch out in his task of exploring the world or asserting his rights as an independent person.

A sense of security can be either shaken or developed in childhood. It is best, if possible, to keep fear, loneliness and anxiety away from our children, so that they can picture their world as a safe place to live in, learning that changes do come but are not always for the worse, that love still surrounds them. What they learn to expect from life will mould their thinking about death and response to loss.

Changes can be survived so long as parents are reliable. Provide security and then the child can usually deal with loss. It requires a careful balance to be sure that a child has all the security he needs and at the same time to avoid being over-protective. He needs the freedom to grow up, to experiment and to make his own mistakes in spite of our carefully phrased advice. In any home there must inevitably be pressures and conflicts as children seek to establish their personhood and find their place in the world, but it is through these battles of the will that a child brings his personality into being. They peak with the temper tantrums of the two-year-old and the rebellions of adolescence.

If you are involved with helping a child who has lost a parent during one of these critical times, remember that the confusion and heartache of bereavement are intensified by the fact that he or she has been left in the middle, as it were, of unfinished business. The child will need help, not only to cope with the pain of loss, but to achieve the sense of identity which is so eagerly sought, especially in adolescence.

The strength of the bond: the price of love

Someone has said that the experience of losing a parent is like finding that the law of gravity has ceased to operate. The bonds of love have been strengthening from before birth and the devastating effect of such a fracture is recognised and understood. However, there are other forms of loss, the pain and repercussions of which may not be recognised.

The lonely person who depends on a dog for companionship will grieve for that pet as for a husband or wife. Forced to leave the family home where they have lived all their lives, an elderly couple will feel that eviction as a bereavement. However, a child who has seen little of a parent during the formative years is less likely to be deeply disturbed.

Loss of brother or sister

It not infrequently happens that in a family where one of the children dies, the effect of this on the others is overlooked because all attention, all the conversation, all the comforting is concentrated on the parents, whose sorrow is the first concern of the family, friends and counsellors.

Yet if, for instance, it is an older brother who has died, the younger one may feel a deep sense of rejection, injustice and anger because no one has recognised the importance of that brother in his life. An older brother or sister can combine the roles of confidant, protector, friend:

> I know from personal experience that bereavement for a child, when they have lost a brother or sister, can be noticeably traumatic and long-lasting.

Not only is the younger child's pain disregarded, but he no longer has his brother to share the feeling of being an outsider from the adult world. In many adolescents this situation can induce thoughts of suicide.[3]

The sorrow of losing a brother or sister can be complicated by memories of quarrels and feelings of envy or jealousy. Sibling rivalry is natural and it is not simply negative. It can carry deep love and admiration. The desire to emulate an older boy or girl can be a spur in achieving goals. Adults can intrude on this relationship by wrongly perceiving it to be based solely on jealousy and making critical comments. In fact siblings love one another in childhood in a way that adults do not always perceive or understand.

When a child is seriously ill and there is a danger of death the other children should be told:

We believed in a healing miracle for Tom, in human terms, and she [his sister] wanted to believe in that too. We didn't prepare Kathryn for the possibility of death, although we spoke openly of how marvellous heaven must be, so when Tom died it was a shock. She was able to see him after he died. This, we feel, was very important. She says we should have warned her he was dying, but also said if she had known, what could she have done – sat at home waiting for it to happen?

Siblings should be allowed and encouraged to share the last days with the dying brother or sister, and to take whatever part is possible in the caring. In this way it should be possible to avoid making the invalid the sole focus of attention, so that the healthy ones, who may not appear to need any regard, feel left out and neglected. That sort of situation can trigger half-formed feelings of jealousy and lead to an intolerable burden of guilt when the invalid dies.[4]

Closer than a brother

Friendships, too, can be as deep and passionate as blood ties, especially in adolescence.

Kelly's best friend, Julie, was killed by a car when they were both sixteen-year-olds at the same school.

I cried and cried. I just couldn't believe she was gone. I kept thinking how full of life she'd been that night, laughing and joking. If Julie and her dad hadn't walked me home they wouldn't have been on that bridge.

I had to go back to school the following week. I felt no one understood. For a long time I stopped doing my school work . . . it took months to get back to normal.

Sometimes I even think I'm going to see her again. Then I remember that I won't and the sadness comes back.

Ben was devastated when his friend Mark committed suicide. They were both at a naval boarding school where Mark was mercilessly bullied.

They'd call him names and trash his room, but he put on a brave face. He shut his feelings inside. I told him he should tell someone but he said not to worry, he'd cope. I left school when I was sixteen but we promised to keep in touch. About three months later I got a call from a boy we'd both known. Mark had killed himself. The night before the new term he went for a walk and never came back. His parents found him hanging from a tree in the garden. He couldn't face going back to the bullies.

I went to pieces. I felt I'd left him to die and was overwhelmed with guilt. I was angry with the bullies, the adults who could have stopped it and even Mark for not asking for help. I became depressed and had lots of bad dreams. I couldn't study so I left college. I lost a stone because I couldn't eat. I felt no one could understand what I was going through. After two months my parents sent me for counselling, which helped. I got out a lot of anger and grief. I had to accept there was nothing I could do about Mark's death.

I think of Mark often. I survived and he didn't and I don't know whether the guilt I feel will ever completely go away.[5]

A very present help: the immediate need and the quality of support

There are long-term dangers of psychiatric disorder following bereavement in childhood, especially after the death of a mother, but these can be lessened considerably where adequate physical and emotional care is given. Children who are supported by relatives, friends, school, church or community, encouraged to talk and cry about their dead parent, freed from guilt feelings and reassured about the future, cope better with their loss.

POINTS TO REMEMBER

**FACTORS THAT MAY AFFECT
A CHILD'S RESPONSE TO LOSS**

- The stability of the home background

- The way death comes

- The closeness of the relationship

- The quality of support at the time

- The personality of the child

- A belief system

3

Poor Jenny is a-weeping: how children mourn

The pain of bereavement, the difficulty of recovering and the possible long-term risks have all been consistently underestimated, and this is particularly true where children are concerned. At one time it was accepted that, whereas adults progress through successive stages of mourning, children would soon forget the lost parent and 'get over' their sorrow. Grief in childhood was, it was assumed, short-lived. Careful observation has revealed that this is not so: little children continue to yearn and weep for the absent parent, especially at bedtime and in the night. The mistaken assumption was due to the fact that the crying child gradually becomes subdued and quieter – but it is the quiet of despair and apathy.

Two-year-olds, parted from their mothers, can become 'beside themselves' with the intensity of their distress, driven frantic with longing for the absent parent: 'He does not know death, but only absence; and if the only person who can satisfy is absent, she might as well be dead, so overwhelming is his sense of loss.'[1]

In adults mourning is an essential step towards recovery from a major loss, by accepting the loss and integrating it with other life experiences. There was a long-lasting controversy as to whether this healing process is possible for small children who lose a parent before they understand the finality of death and the full extent of their loss. Some considered that mourning could not take place before adolescence, when the breaking of parental bonds itself constitutes an initiation into how to mourn. However, it seems likely that children of any age are capable of mourning, but that there may be a greater risk of pathological reactions because of their limited understanding.

Misunderstanding

There is no doubt that children do suffer deeply, sometimes into adulthood, when a parent dies, but adults may often mistake their reactions and not realise what they are going through. There are several reasons for this. As teachers find, children have a short concentration span and their attention moves rapidly from one activity to another. They are likely to break off their weeping and turn to play, until some need reminds them that Mummy or Daddy is not there. Some children will express their grief through bouts of unusually strenuous activity; or they may find a listening ear and be able to talk about it; they may be able to approach the subject only through play, or they may seek relief of anger by thumping another child!

Many children are very sensitive to a parent's feelings and try not to add to the burden by sharing their sorrow. They hide their heartache: 'I can't talk to Mummy about it because it makes her cry'; but in doing so they may be thought unfeeling. This can lead to a difficult situation in which the child is afraid to upset the parent and the parent is then afraid to upset the child, fearing it will make things worse. It may need the good sense of some friend or relative to break the deadlock and get them talking. In 1977 Dr Dora Black set up a family therapy service, using trained social workers, with the specific aim of opening communication between parents and children and facilitating the mourning process. Use was made of drawing materials and toys where younger children were involved. These methods have proved very helpful in enabling children to grieve.

Children have great difficulty in coping with the demands of working through grief and at the same time overcoming the effects of traumatic experiences (as at Dunblane). It appears that efforts at relieving traumatic anxiety take psychological priority

over mourning. This may be a further cause of family misunderstandings as, for example, when grief-stricken relatives
fail to appreciate the child's apparent inability to grieve with the
same intensity as they themselves are feeling.[2]

It's not true!

Children's mourning is different from adults' in that while
mourning in adults makes it possible for them to become
gradually detached from their relationship with the dead
person, children can carry two pictures in their mind at the
same time. They really know that their parent is dead, but they
refuse to accept the fact. Their minds are protecting them from
the pain, allowing them to continue in their 'inner world' a
relationship with the person who has been lost in the real world:

> The children talked easily about their father, particularly the
> little ones of three and four who made an imaginary
> companion of him as some children will invent a playmate.
> They made room for him on the sofa, saved cakes for him and
> included him in all their games.
> By talking about him in this uninhibited way, the children
> seemed to spare themselves the complete emptiness some
> children suffer through learning to feel – and to say – 'I have
> no father.'[3]

In recent years, we have begun to understand the critical
importance of childhood experiences for later life. It appears
that separation anxiety in small children parted from their
mothers is similar to types of unhealthy mourning in the
adult, which may happen when children are not allowed to
express their grief at the time of the loss.

Alex lost her mother when she was three years old:

> I don't know whether a different handling of my emotions as
> a child would have made any difference to me, but I suppose
> it might. My father, from the best motives and a desire to

spare me, never told me that my mother had died, and never spoke of her. This, I am sure, is wrong. Before anything else a young child must be allowed to grieve in full. I can't stress too much that, however painful it may be to the remaining adults, they must encourage the child to experience the agony of loss.

Unfortunately adults cannot face the pain of heartbroken children and their knee-jerk reaction is to try and stop them talking about it. The findings of those engaged on relief work during the disasters of Zeebrugge and Hillsborough revealed an almost universal lack of appreciation of the child's understanding, with people talking over their heads, and a general reluctance to talk with children or give them the opportunity to express their feelings freely.

The first weeks of life

During the first few weeks of life while babies are not aware of themselves as persons separate from their mother, they will miss her predominantly as the one who has provided their physical needs, food and warmth and comfort, and the urgent requirement is to find a reliable caring substitute mother for them. There is of course more to it than that. The process of bonding relies heavily on the sense of touch and smell, and the baby will know the feeling and smell of his mother's familiar body. A mother cannot easily be replaced. Moreover, we now know much more about the development of the baby in the womb and the unborn child's sensitivity to his mother's frame of mind and emotional state. For a child so recently emerged from the womb, her death must mean more than a physical loss. We should not be surprised if the catastrophe has some later outcome, as in Nigel's experience:

I was in my mother's womb when she caught puerperal fever, which also infected me so that I nearly died at birth. My mother contracted peritonitis at this time, and this resulted in her death about a month after I was born. I was well into my

teens before my father decided to tell me briefly that my
mother had died shortly after my birth. Many years later,
when I was well on the way to recovering from a nervous
breakdown, my father decided to tell me the circumstances of
my mother's death and the illnesses in greater detail. By this
time I had begun to realise that these early traumatic
experiences had had a profound effect upon my start in life.

I think there were two main effects upon me of my
mother's death, which I only became aware of many years
later, and after prayer. These were:

   i)   the fear of death, and
   ii) the fear of being abandoned by the one I was most
        dependent upon.

These fears, I believe, had a crippling effect upon my
emotional development, and I grew up into adult life, and
even into marriage, not really knowing how to love others:
only what it is like to be on the receiving end of it.

Jenny Marshall was also an infant when her mother died, so
she grew up knowing little or nothing about her. All through her
childhood years and into adulthood she suffered the oppression
of a constant overshadowing grief. She knew no reason for this,
and assumed that such a state was normal experience.

I lost my mother when I was two weeks old and therefore I
believe that I must really have sensed the separation, and
maybe it has affected me. I've had quite a lot of prayer for it –
for deep healing – so that memory could be – not forgotten,
for we aren't designed to forget – but healed. I used to feel a
terrible sense of grief, and I didn't know what it was until I
went to a priest, a Catholic monk, who had a healing ministry
and he prayed that the memory would be healed.

The best we can do for children bereaved at this age is to
provide continuity of care, which includes provision for their
physical needs to relieve anxiety, and constancy of affection as
an antidote to fear.

Searching and pining

I suppose I grieved for him, but I don't remember. I do remember pining for him and also looking for his body. I felt sure it must be hidden somewhere. I looked secretly, understanding that this would upset my parents. He wasn't under my bed or under his. Neither was he in the airing cupboard. I probably looked in other places too.

By the time they are two years old babies are able to recognise the people in their world and can call up a mental image of someone who is absent, an ability which the mourning process requires. As soon as they can picture their mother they will miss her presence and are likely to search for her obsessively. They will need to be assured over and over again that she will not return, for they cannot understand the permanence of their loss.

When she does not return they might show distress by crying and protesting and calling for her, by going off their food and losing interest in their toys and activities, by pining and then apathy. They can be helped by keeping the sort of routine going to which they had been used before their mother died. A familiar pattern of living can reduce the unsettling effect of some inevitable changes and constant loving care will help them to adapt to the new situation.

Multiple losses

Children can really deal with only one event or issue at a time and can be very confused when there are several changes in the family at once.

Mary was delighted when a little brother, Matthew, (a premature baby) arrived to complete the family of four.

When he died six weeks later she was devastated. She had already suffered two significant losses and told everyone that he was 'in heaven' with 'Muzzie' (her grandmother) and Punch (her grandmother's dog, who had accidentally hanged himself in the car). Mary went to Matthew's funeral, but was taken out during the service. She showed her distress in two ways:

i)   She refused to play with her doll. It was dead.
ii) She began to cry inconsolably at night, unable to say why.

The health visitor diagnosed that she was 'stuck' in her grief, and referral was made to the Child Guidance team, where Mary was rapidly helped.

Against professional advice Mary's parents decided to have another baby to be close to Mary, and a calendar was made to mark off the days 'until the new baby comes'. Mary became very confused and asked if Matthew was coming back. She frequently asked the health visitor to look at Matthew's photograph album with her and found it helpful, so they decided to buy another album, one for Mary, one for Matthew and one for 'our new baby'.

Mary was full of fear: if her father disappeared for a while she would ask if he was dead. From the beginning we had to be careful to say 'Goodbye' if we left the house. Now we had to be more so. She had lost her 'Muzzie', Punch and her brother in six months, and she was only two and a half. Death was very much part of her life. Whenever she was particularly sad or anxious Mary would ask to visit Matthew's grave. She did not know that his body was there, but liked to take flowers 'to remember him'.

The first year passed and Victoria, a healthy baby, was born, but anxiety and visits to the grave were frequent. Victoria's album began to fill, but Mary always referred to her as 'this baby' and frequently asked if she was going to die.

By the time Mary was at school, Matthew had been dead three and a half years, another baby, James, had been born and the family had moved house. This makes a difficult time for a five-year-old: three significant losses, the arrival of two more siblings to challenge her place and a house move, with consequent loss of friends.

Personality change

Mary's reaction suggests that she is suffering from the loss of self-esteem that often occurs in bereavement and can produce changes of personality. Mandy, another five-year-old whose baby brother died, 'behaved quite appropriately at the time' crying and clinging, waking in the night complaining of ghosts, and then seemed to settle down and cope by becoming well behaved and helpful around the house.

The health visitor in charge of the case wrote:

Suddenly her behaviour began to change. She became increasingly bad-tempered and was rude to her parents and everyone around her. She became disruptive at school and wouldn't eat her meals. She was violent at home and wouldn't go to bed. Fourteen months had passed since the baby's death, and the parents had made it clear that they didn't want to talk about it. They didn't want to be reminded of their loss. No one ever mentioned the baby and his pictures were put away in a drawer. The house became tatty and the children often missed school. The slow collapse of the family's routine spelled out the problem of unresolved grief. It needed the sensitivity of someone who understood to bring out and confront the situation by saying openly that the baby's name was never mentioned and his pictures had been hidden. Glances of fear between the family rapidly turned to red-hot anger (which seemed to rage for hours) as I became the focus for all the family's pain, isolation, rage and betrayal.

At last the little girl whispered to me, 'Will you take me home with you?' I asked her why, and she told me: 'Mummy doesn't love me. She loves Julian [the dead baby] more.' So I asked her mother if she did, and she began to cry, shaking her head slowly and sadly. The tears flowed down her face – sad tears this time, not angry ones as before.

'*Do* you love Mandy?' I asked. She nodded, the only sign that the little girl needed to run to her. I left them that day with their arms around one another, sobbing out the grief that should have been cast away so many months before.

Although life began to improve for this family Mandy's behaviour still showed signs of inner disturbance. It was discovered that she wanted to see the place where the baby was buried and was afraid that they had forgotten where he was. She hadn't liked to ask her mum and dad to take her to the grave because 'it makes Daddy cry'.

So on a bitter winter's day they made their way fearfully to the cemetery. The grass had been clipped and tidied up a bit and Mum had put a few flowers in a jam jar by the hedge. Small though this gesture was, it indicated that they acknowledged a responsibility for the baby and accepted him as part of the family.

It was not until they were home that Mandy was finally able to exorcise her grief:

I have never seen – and I hope I shall never see again – such suffering as I saw in that child that day. Her grief, so long repressed, tore from her like nothing I have seen before and wrenched her body into contortions in its savagery. She screamed a sound like an animal and howled before the spasm finally called to an end what she had been feeling.

Children share with adults the emotions they feel in bereavement, and as they grow in their understanding of death and approach adolescence their ways of expressing them also become similar. Common reactions are fear, anger and guilt.

Fear

Bereaved children are often oppressed by fear: they may have nightmares and various irrational anxieties: they may fear losing their surviving parent, and if they have reached an age when they understand the universal nature of death, they may fear their own. When Tony was six, his father was killed by a bomb. His mother wrote: 'Tony would cling to me, becoming hysterical if I was out of his sight. He became very withdrawn and would not speak. Of course, this made school very difficult.'

Often bereaved children become obsessed with accidents, illness or death, particularly with regard to their lone parent or siblings. Peggy, whose father drowned at sea, had dreadful disturbing nightmares, seeing her room filling up with water. They may be afraid to go to sleep, especially if they have heard death spoken of in metaphor as 'sleep', or of a pet being 'put to sleep'. A study of pre-pubescent bereaved children has shown that many experience suicidal feelings, though without corresponding suicidal behaviour.[3]

Anger

Girls aged seven and ten reacted differently to the death of their father:

> One flew into fits of anger, especially when I had to go out and leave her. I had a battle to get her to allow me to go out in the car. In hindsight I see she had a fear that I too may crash and not return home.

Fear and anger are associated feelings, and in the turmoil of this confusion children may behave in a way that produces an undesired contrary outcome. They may be yearning for sympathy but drive it away:

> When Karen's mother died of cancer she became obstinate and awkward. She thought, 'How could God do this to me? I hate God!' Then when her father died less than a year later she became physically violent to everything and everyone around her.

Anger derives from the need to find someone to blame and is often directed against the surviving parent: 'Why are you still here, and not Dad? Why did you let him die?' When Marion's husband was drowned she wrote, 'I definitely did not know how to cope with the children's anger that was directed against me.' But her son Stephen, who was fourteen, blamed another frequent target: 'It's not fair. God could have saved my dad. He stilled the rough seas in the Bible. He's not a very nice God.'

There is good evidence that the most intense emotion experienced by bereaved children is rage rather than grief. When anger is turned on to themselves, it becomes guilt.

Guilt

It is common for children of any age to blame themselves when a parent dies. At about four they reach what is called the age of 'magical thinking', when they feel responsible for what happens in the world of which they are the centre. When a parent dies they may remember having been disobedient or at some time saying, without meaning it, 'I wish you were dead', and when this happens they blame themselves. When a sibling dies they are especially vulnerable because of natural rivalry, or jealousy when a new baby arrives to take some of the attention which has been exclusively theirs.

Older children blame themselves for real misdemeanours, rebellion and misunderstandings:

> When I was thirteen Mother became ill. Dad asked me would I mind if she came home in a wheelchair. The suggestion shocked me and I felt No! I couldn't stand the stares of other people. Then Mother died the next week and I was over-loaded with guilt for years afterwards, convinced that that had some effect on her death, my wicked thoughts!

Action

What can be done to help bereaved children to avoid psychological and social difficulties in the future? Children will often bottle up their feelings and may show less ability to express their hurts than adults. This may be because they cannot verbalise their emotions and may need an adult's help to express and overcome their sorrow, rage or distress. Yet adults, especially in Western cultures, fear the grief of children and will shy away from giving such opportunities. One letter suggests: 'They should be encouraged to talk about their dead parents. They will not take the initiative if they are of a certain age.' It may be another child with whom they can be open and honest.

- Talk – the relief of emotional stress through talking and weeping is one of the most important helps towards recovery.

- Good physical and emotional care are essential throughout childhood, with a watchful eye for what happens at school with regard both to academic progress and to relationships with other children and staff members.

- Children of school age are generally capable of being helped towards an understanding of death, and this is a first step towards developing a healthy attitude towards it. For example, a simple explanation of the possible causes would relieve children of the burden created by thinking that their careless words might have been responsible.

- Children who are 'stuck' in their grief or who have anxieties and fears may need specialised help from those who understand the thinking of children and can talk with them in ways they will understand.

- Those who are caring for bereaved children also need support, for the child's eventual outcome is related to the way their surviving parent or caretaker is able to cope with their own grief and changed circumstances.

- It is advisable to minimise secondary changes, especially those involving further disruption of family ties, e.g. separation of siblings. The need for the familiar is so strong that any unnecessary change in the early weeks, e.g. change of school, should be avoided.

POINTS TO REMEMBER

WATCH OUT FOR POSSIBLE MISUNDERSTANDING

- Children do not always react to sorrow as adults do. We need to be sensitive to their pain and realise that they may be suffering more than they show.

- Children are very thoughtful in their desire to spare their parents' feelings and will sometimes hide their grief for that reason.

- Children can be affected by a mother's death from a very early age and suffer the effects in adulthood.

- A child may search obsessively for a parent who has died, and show separation anxiety.

- Children may show distress by becoming confused, withdrawn or disruptive, or by a change in personality.

- Children must be given the opportunity of attending the funeral and joining in all family mourning.

- Children must be given the opportunity of talking about their loss.

WHAT DO THEY NEED?

- Good physical and emotional care.

- A clear understanding of what has happened.

- For some children specialist care may be needed to resolve problems.

- Carers may also need support.

4

Broken lives:
'My world's gone wrong'

Sombre prospect

In Britain in 1994 there were:

200,000 ch:ldren who had lost parents by death
160,000 children who had lost parents through divorce
100,000 children whose parents were in prison, of whom 96
per cent were men and 4 per cent women.

One in every eight families with children is now headed by a
single parent.

These statistics mean that there is a sizeable proportion of
children living in a world that must seem to have gone badly
wrong. These different types of deprivation are linked by
common strands running through them. Whether it comes
through death or by divorce or as a result of imprisonment,
the absence of a parent from a child's world means the withdrawal of a source of authority, protection and comfort. The
loss diminishes a child's resources for facing life and entails
further losses.

Loss of trust

The sense of trust is the keystone of personality and forms the
base on which we make lasting relationships. Bereavement can

shake and damage this essential trait, so that children may grow feeling that they can never again put their faith in anything or anybody.

Loss of self-esteem

Children who lose a parent also lose the state of well-being that was inherent in the relationship of love and trust. The special bond with all it meant in terms of personal worth is broken, and while it can be seen that no one can help dying, it is more difficult to accept that he or she has chosen to leave and make another home, especially when other children follow. Children blame themselves either way, and feel they must have done something to precipitate the situation. The bereaved children of Hiroshima plaintively wondered why – 'we hadn't done anything wrong and yet our parents died'. Children of divorce are shut out and feel devalued: 'I can't be worth much!' And they may grow up with the inner conviction that they are unlovable. There is similar heartache when a parent goes to prison and the whole family bears the stigma of rejection.

Each situation carries its own pain – the finality of death, the divided loyalties and conflict of divorce, the shame of prison – and all may mean that the whole pattern of life must change with disorientating suddenness.

Effects of grief

Physical – children may show physical signs of distress. They may tire very easily and show their distress in a strained appearance and vacant look. They may have frequent tummy aches and revert to baby ways such as wetting the bed, thumb-sucking and clinging. Adolescents may lose interest in their appearance and neglect themselves. They may search for the dead loved one, returning again and again to some place where he might once have been seen.

Emotional – they may become emotionally unstable with sudden mood swings of anger, guilt, pining, fear and depression, feeling lost.

Although Sally seemed to cope at the time, it later emerged that she hadn't. During some very difficult times in her teenage years she said, 'Nobody thought that I missed Daddy. I loved him too, but you were all concerned about Tony.'

Educational – lack of concentration and anxiety may make children unable to work, especially at exam times. They may be unable to remember what they should be doing and feel they cannot face school and their friends. This may result in school avoidance and truancy. Bereaved children should be warned that their progress at school may be affected, and helped to handle their problems:

The only immediate effect of my mother's death was that having been first or second in the 2nd year, I then went down to thirtieth in the 3rd year. Being told that it was natural to drop in position at school would have helped.

Behavioural – children who can't express themselves in words make their feelings known by the way they behave. They may have uncharacteristic angry outbursts or over-react to small upsets; previously friendly children may become aggressive and stroppy in school, unwilling to take part in activities. They have a great need to feel that they can hurt others as they have been hurt themselves, 'paying back', as it were, and disruptive behaviour is one of the commonest symptoms of grief, especially unresolved grief. Delinquency carries its own irrational logic – stealing to restore a loss, vandalism to destroy in return for destruction, aggression to 'get back' at someone or something.

Because of Tony's behavioural problems at school, they talked of sending him to a 'special unit'. I considered this totally the wrong thing for him.

There may be a more ominous side to this, especially in older children who may take to using stimulants or other drugs. And there are some who may take desperate measures involving self-harm, perhaps through inflicting pain on themselves in extreme throes of guilt or through the remorseless, slow starvation of anorexia nervosa.

Psychological – states of mind may include anxiety, panic attacks and a fear of being 'the next on the list' to die. There may be long-lasting depression, in which nothing seems worth doing because the sense of identity is lost and the child feels isolated in a bad place – a 'broken world'.

High risk factors

Age-related risk

There is a connection between the age at which children are bereaved and problems later in life if grief is not resolved. One study found that 'there is a higher incidence of depressive illness in adults who lose a parent before the age of 10 than in those whose parents live longer'.[1] In another, 'most of the depressed patients experienced bereavement before the age of 4; a smaller number between 5 and 9; the smallest number between 10 and 14'.[2]

The risk is greater to children under the age of five, who have as yet no understanding of death, for without that realisation the child cannot complete the task of mourning.

Death of the same-sex parent

Every individual makes for himself a picture of what he is and what he would like to be and sets up ideals for his strivings.[3]

Parents are crucial in this business of making a picture of oneself. As parents we are being watched all the time: the boys are taking note of what it means to be a man like Dad and the girls are taking note of what Mum is and does. Not only this, but the boys are considering that the girl they will marry must be like Mum and the girls will look to Dad for a picture of their future partner in life.

It is always devastating when a parent dies, for the children lose their role model of what they will become and their mental image of whom they may marry. It is the loss of the same-sex parent that damages the process of forming a self-image, one of the elements of self-esteem, and it is therefore the death of a mother that makes growing up difficult for a girl and the death of a father for a boy.

This is borne out by the fact that a higher rate of delinquency has been found in children who have had to live with the opposite-sex parent alone. Waveney Holt lost her mother when she was thirteen and suffered serious effects of delayed grief in adult life. She wrote, 'I feel it would have helped if there had been a female presence around to help get out the bottled-up feelings inside me.'

Having to live with their mothers alone seems to hit adolescent boys particularly hard. A CRUSE leaflet says: 'Of bereaved in the community the very depressed bereaved children seem to be mostly boys who have lost their fathers.'

Boys of violent fathers are also particularly vulnerable, for their attachment to their mother may conflict with their formation of a male identity, as they recognise her plight and feel moved to identify with her in her fearful situation.[4]

Change in circumstances

Following her husband's death Marion wrote:

Two weeks ago I bought and moved into a new house, just two miles from our old one, where we had lived for ten and a half years. I knew that I would live in the past for ever if I stayed in the house where Chris had been with us. I was totally unprepared for the way we reacted. Peggy was sad, but she has her own home now so it was less traumatic for her.

Roy was very sad, Stephen almost inconsolable and I cried all day.

One loss at a time is hard to bear, but a parent's death often brings other related losses. Having to move house in the middle of a major grief is in itself another bereavement, especially if it is a place where the family has lived for many years and children have grown up. Financial constraints may make this unavoidable, and it may involve changing school, less pocket money and therefore a loss in status, and losing friends and the old familiar places.

Jack was killed by the IRA bomb in Regent's Park on 20 July 1982.

Jack's death meant that the children lost not only a father, but all their friends as well. All their lives till then had been with the Army. In one moment all that they'd known had been wiped out.

When a father dies a family may break up completely and children may have to go into care or be found foster homes. Sometimes a surviving parent may take another partner, and though in some cases this may be the best solution, in others it can sometimes be bitterly resented by the children:

Three years later, when I was sixteen, Dad met someone else, complete opposite of Mum, a hairdresser, blonde, divorcée, with two girls younger than me. To begin with this new family was quite fun. It was war-time and she lived in Kingston, so my father got 'digs' there and I was put to live with them. (They didn't actually marry for another three or four years.) It proved a very traumatic time for me – she didn't hit me, but her tongue was very cruel.

Previous damage

A child who has had unhappy experiences in the past has lowered resistance to the damage of parental loss. This applies to an unstable background, for instance one where there has been conflict, separation or divorce, and also to children who have been physically or sexually abused. The dented self-esteem makes them vulnerable to depression in adult life.

The outsider

Children who are excluded from the funeral and family discussions, who do not know what is going on and have received no effectual communication about their parent's death are left in a state of bewilderment and fear. If no one speaks to them about what has happened they may get the idea that it is something they should not talk about. It is most unwise to repress feelings in this way. Adults may feel that they should protect children from pain and tragedy, but children intuitively know that something important and terrible has happened. Sometimes people say of a child of perhaps five or six years old, 'I don't think he really knows what has happened', which shows a sad lack of understanding on the part of the adult. Children are at their most intuitive at this age. The mental constraints that children can endure when they feel isolated from the rest of the family can bring unfortunate results in later life:

I never felt 'included' in the death, it wasn't talked about enough to me. I felt lost but didn't know how to ask grown-ups how Mum was. I was told of my mother's death by a boy in the playground at school. He must have overheard a telephone conversation and told me laughingly, 'Your mummy is dead.' I pushed it down but can still feel the utter loneliness of walking back into school, sitting cross-legged on a wooden floor in a half-moon round the piano. I knew then that Mummy had died. I was taken home and remember feeling no emotion at all. It wasn't until I was twenty-one that I actually cried with my father about the death. I didn't attend the funeral. I have no recollection of being given any reassurance. The problem was that I cut myself off from the pain by not talking about Mum at all.

Coping alone

The outcome for bereaved children must depend to a large extent on the ability of the surviving parent to cope with the whole situation. This will mean her own grief and disorientation, the running of the home, possibly reduced circumstances and finding time to help the children deal with their sorrow and their problems. This is a time when we realise how much we have lost in the extended family of days gone by, when it would have been taken for granted that grandparents, aunts and uncles and cousins would rally round to lift some of the burden from the lone parent. It is possible to feel reluctant to ask for help from neighbours and friends ('I don't like to impose on them'), but they too may hold back, fearing to intrude, though they would be glad to do some of the chores, leaving the widowed parent time to talk with and comfort the children. One mother was so harassed by domestic day-to-day concerns, together with things like tax returns and responsibilities that her husband used to handle, that she had no idea what the children were going through:

Both children reacted differently. One flew into fits of anger, especially when I had to go out and leave her. My younger child withdrew and in many ways suffered more – because she was so quiet no one took any notice. Her progress at school came to a halt yet again. It wasn't seen at the time; only years later was it realised by her immaturity. What I am trying to say in all this is that I had no idea of the danger signs. The signals my children were sending out were ignored, not wilfully, but simply not recognised. I didn't know how to work through grief with my children by spending time with them, talking, maybe just sitting quietly with them. I was so determined to get through a day at a time and relieved when I did so.

Sudden, unexpected or violent death

Special dangers attach to deaths caused by violence or disaster, which are by their nature horrifying and deeply upsetting. The distress they inflict is even greater when it is caused by the anger or intentional malice of people than when it is the result of some natural phenomenon, however cataclysmic. For example, the emotional damage is greater from witnessing a parent's murder than from being involved in an earthquake. The psychological shock is in the same order as that experienced by soldiers suffering from shell shock in the First World War, or from battle experience such as Goose Green. Ways that are appropriate for coping with everyday stresses are overwhelmed and inadequate for the scale of the catastrophe and its emotional repercussion. War brings agonising losses, which traumatise not only the soldiers themselves, but also widows and children who participate in their agony, perhaps through visualising the fate of men trapped in a blazing hold or perhaps in trying to nurse a shattered body back to some semblance of life. Children will even relive the scenes in which their fathers died and suffer nightmares as though they had actually witnessed them.

Until as recently as 1985 it was thought that children were less affected than adults by witnessing horrific scenes, but the fact is that children suffer traumatic stress symptoms which are unrecognised or underestimated by the adults in their lives. When the *Herald of Free Enterprise* sank off Zeebrugge in 1987, the psychologists asked to assess the children involved found difficulties similar to those found by Michael Stewart, the chief psychotherapist in charge of the counselling after the Bradford fire. Both met reluctance on the part of the adults to admit the severity of the emotional disturbance suffered by the children.

> In part, it is because adults are understandably very protective towards children who have suffered a disaster; and in part it is because adults, unwilling to acknowledge what children may have suffered, deny that children have major sequelae that warrant investigation.[5]

Children who witness the violent death of a parent suffer stress symptoms including flashbacks and dreams that re-enact the horror they have seen. It is interesting to note that traumatic reactions like this can interfere with the grieving process, for grieving requires you to remember while traumatic stress victims want to forget.

Adolescence

There are so many physical and emotional changes going on in the life of an adolescent that a loss of the magnitude of a parent's death coming at this time has the destructive power of a bombshell. There is good evidence to suggest that they grieve in a similar way to adults, but that they often do so privately and do not turn to the school or relatives for help. There may be reasons for this – maybe they fear being misunderstood, even by their peers; they may not know how to cope with their emotions, or they may feel that they must be strong for the sake of a grieving parent.

One mother whose husband was lost at sea felt that the loss of a father comes particularly hard on the adolescent. Soon after the drowning, her two sons, aged fourteen and sixteen, were arrested for making nuisance calls on neighbours; and while they were waiting for definite news of their dad the eldest boy would ride his bike carelessly round the streets, thinking that if he were to be killed it would save his dad. In his mind he was striking a bargain – his death in exchange for his father's life.

Adolescents are in the process of breaking parental bonds and establishing a new identity, no longer as a child but as an adult. This will mean letting go of childhood and of the authority and protection of the parent, beginning to take on family responsibilities themselves. It is important that they do not feel pressured to take on more than they are ready for, but at the same time it must be remembered that the shouldering of reasonable responsibility can help the working out of grief. They will have to adjust to different relationships, and will want to know how the death will affect them. Will it blight their university hopes, their career prospects?

Humpty Dumpty

The effects of parental loss in childhood may not emerge until many years later and may take various forms.

Delayed grief

When I was thirteen my mother became ill and died in hospital . . . there had been no family doctor to talk to, no clergy. I had enormous difficulty with bereavement, my father was unsociable and had practically no friends.

Fifty-four years later, after watching *Shadowlands*, tears were pouring down my face and would not stop . . . I decided the people in the film had succeeded in doing what I and Dad had never done – grieved together happily. A few weeks later I had a vivid dream. I and my father (who appeared as he was in his forties) were going for a walk together at the seaside and our relationship was right back to where it had been in my early teens and we were content in each other's company.

My parents died within a short time of each other when I was six years old, and I believe that even now, at the age of forty, I grieve for them.

Relationship problems

'We were a family of four when my mother died. My father would be about thirty, I was five and my brother would have been three. Dad admits now that the death wasn't handled well for John and me. The grief and unanswered questions I carried for all those years were pushed deep down and my smile and happy disposition covered a tremendous hurt which I was unable to voice to anyone . . . I feel sure all the problems I have had stem from losing my mum at an early age and not being allowed to grieve.' Gail, who wrote this, had two marriages which both ended in divorce, and her children now live apart from her with their father.

Physical illness and neuroses

When I was eleven years old my father died suddenly with no warning in the hallway of our house . . . When I was about thirty-four I became ill. I lived in a daze, losing concentration easily – most uncharacteristic. I had tightness around the throat all the time. I slept badly with vivid dreams. I woke in the morning terrified and panic-stricken . . . Eventually I saw a doctor who made me go through the events of the day my father died in great detail. When I left the surgery it was like being born again. A weight had lifted. The world was bright again.

Suicide

My mother died when I was thirteen . . . I did not grieve at all – my father was a very silent man who just got on, and so did I. Strangely though, I really felt the effects of my mother's death in April 1982, seven years after my father's death in 1975. As far as I can gather, when my mother died I just transferred all my affection to my father . . . Finally, however, the underlying never-acknowledged grief began to surface. A few terrible months culminated in my taking an overdose – and on coming round after four days I said, 'I want my Mummy'. So twenty-three years after the death I was able to grieve for my mother.

There is reasonable hope of healing the wounds if attention is paid to the needs of bereaved children at the time of their parent's death. Ways of doing this are explored in the next chapter.

POINTS TO REMEMBER

POSSIBLE EFFECTS OF PARENTAL DEATH

- Loss of self-esteem
- Damage to sense of trust
- Manifestation of grief — physical, emotional, educational, behavioural, psychological
- Teenagers may become suicidal. Don't think that people who threaten suicide don't do it. Some do. GET HELP

HIGH-RISK FACTORS FOR GRIEF-RELATED PROBLEMS

- Age-related risk
- Death of same-sex parent
- Changes in circumstances following the death, e.g. moving house
- Previous unhappy experience, e.g. broken home
- Exclusion from funeral and family mourning
- Poor coping ability of surviving parent
- Sudden, unexpected or violent death

5

Bind up the broken-hearted: limiting the damage

> . . . the thousand natural shocks
> That flesh is heir to. (*Hamlet III:i:56*)

The media today present a worldwide picture of children left parentless for one reason or another: starvation on a global scale, natural disasters, disease and domestic violence. Bearing in mind the intercontinental spread of AIDS and escalating conflicts in many places it seems likely that there will be a continuing and growing need to address the problems these children face.

What can be done?

Much can be deduced from the unhappy circumstances already outlined. Measures to limit the damage of childhood bereavement may be considered in three stages:

 i) Pre-emptive help
 ii) Urgent help
 iii) Crisis avoidance

Pre-emptive help

> All that live must die,
> Passing through nature to eternity. (*Hamlet I:ii:70*)

In spite of all the media coverage and counselling advice given during recent major tragedies there is still a consistent natural tendency to eliminate the idea of death from our consciousness. Children are not prepared, either by formal education or by their daily observation of life, for the impact of grief on our lives. It is essentially part of our Western culture to cherish the illusion that some people die – but not us.

A first step in the prevention of bereavement-related psychiatric disorders must be to sweep away the taboo and allow death to enter our thinking as a stage in the continuum of our existence. In the wake of Dunblane there has been renewed enthusiasm in school circles for guidelines which would include open communication and ideas for 'death in the classroom', but despite this the undercover message that gets across is that we avoid the subject if we possibly can. The message, even for little children, should be that no one has yet been born who has not died. This is an important point, for even as young as five years old children can be helped to realise the finality of death, without which they are not equipped to mourn. They can also learn about the many causes of death, which would relieve them of the burden of thinking their angry thoughts had killed someone, and could help to make them aware of the more obvious ways of avoiding accidents.

Pre-emptive measures will be considered further in Chapter 8.

Urgent help

Help of an urgent nature is called for when a child is giving out mayday signals in the form of disturbed behaviour, or when it is known that she or he has suffered some traumatic experience that should receive immediate action in the form of debriefing by an expert. Symptoms of such a condition might take the form of persistent replays of the scenes witnessed or constantly repeated horrific dreams. Fears may rise to the surface that need specific help from those who have experience and training in understanding children's ways of thought and communicating at their level.

Bereavement counselling generally, in particular the family intervention introduced by Dr Dora Black, has been found to be beneficial to adults and there are now strategies that can reduce the distress of children at the time of their loss, and so lessen the likelihood of depression in the future.

This is the province of specialists, but it is relevant for all those who have the care of children to be on the lookout for signs of stress, to be aware of what help is available and to know when to seek such help in consultation with a social worker, GP, pastor or other professional.

When to seek further professional help

Watch out for:[1]

- Persistent anxieties about own death

- Destructive outbursts

- Euphoria

- Accident prone-ness

- Unwillingness to speak of the dead person

- Expression of *only* negative or *only* positive feelings about the deceased

- Inability or unwillingness to form new relationships

- Daydreaming – poor academic progress

- Stealing

- School phobia

Crisis avoidance

The object of pre-emptive help is to give children some defensive mechanism for coping with parental loss before it happens, while specialist help may be needed in some serious situation, such as that following a disaster which has left a child traumatised, or the witnessing of a parent's murder.[2]

It is in the third of our divisions that the majority of parents, teachers, clergy and friends are most likely to be able to help. However, anyone taking on such a responsibility should reckon on the possibility of needing support themselves. The outcome for the child is strongly related to the way the adult carers are able, at the same time, to cope with both their own grief and that of the child.

What does the child need?

- Openness: reliable information and truthful answers
- Reassurance: structure, routine and authority
- Freedom: space, free expression of emotion
- Inclusion: a sense of belonging
- Understanding and comfort

Openness

> Give sorrow words: the grief that does not speak
> Whispers the o'er-fraught heart and bids it break
> (*Macbeth IV:iii:208*)

It is not always possible to tell what a child is feeling or to predict how he may be affected in later life. Often it is possible only years later to see the result of mistakes made at the time. One of the most frequent of these is the failure to give children an adequate truthful explanation of what has happened, and what is going on in the adult world, though this is often for the kindest of motives. In his guidelines for setting up a child bereavement counselling service, Rev. Nigel Copsey wrote:

> The adults spent the time trying to protect the child rather than trying to understand the child's world, with the result that the child was not allowed to mourn and found it hard to trust later.[3]

Information should be explicit unless there is reliable professional advice to the contrary; if, for example, the child has been told that death has been caused by a heart attack but later discovers that it was suicide, the grief may resurface, bringing a surplus of later problems.

The reasons for this failure may be practical. The surviving parent may be distraught and unable to cope, and all the focus of attention may be on her, so the children get overlooked. If necessary it is important to find some sensible, trusted friend or relative to take on this sensitive task of informing the children.

The major tragedies of the last few years have revealed that the usual adult reaction is still to try to hide what has happened, especially from younger children. They may be told some improbable story (for example, 'Daddy has gone on a business trip') which they will know is a lie, and feel that, in addition to the mystery of the missing parent, they are surrounded by unreliable adults. David, whose father was killed by a direct hit on the house during the Blitz, was not told what had happened to his father till years later.

After the Bradford fire Michael Stewart, the chief psychotherapist, wrote:

> Parents and teachers are extremely reluctant to face the problem of childhood bereavement with the result that children are 'shielded from pain' and this, as you probably appreciate, is a very grave error of judgement . . . I suggested, following the disaster, a seminar involving parents and teachers as well as the children. The response was one of horror! This indicates to me that it is the teachers who need help.

The follow-up from major disasters such as the *Herald of Free Enterprise* suggests that parents are not always the most reliable or observant reporters of their children's reactions.

Yet consideration for the children is not the only obstacle to free communication. Adults are often embarrassed and tongue-tied ('People stop talking when I go into the room') and try to avoid having to cope with a child's questions that they cannot answer or with reactions they cannot help. Naturally parents may have difficulty in talking about the death because it brings their own sorrow to the surface with renewed force. However, as we have seen from the previous unhappy case histories, one of the vital factors in warding off later problems is to tell children the truth at the time, however difficult this may be.

Reassurance: structure, routine and authority

When their world falls apart and there is no one to establish boundaries or take Dad's role as law-giver, children are very much in need of the reassurance that a structure can give to their lives. Keep to any daily routines already in place in the home and maintain the everyday rules for organising life. Most families have some habits and agreed ways of doing things: mealtimes make good opportunities to get together and share any problems. One family found it helpful to have a regular prayer time together:

> One of the most important things we did, as I look back, was when we started as a family reserving a part of each day where we could share the Scripture together and pray together. We started doing this as a regular habit in the morning after breakfast, so it became part of our daily routine. So when we had our tragedy we just carried on. It seemed to be the natural thing to do.

It is reassuring if there are some things that stay the same.

Freedom: space, free expression of emotion

Children and adolescents who are struggling with intense emotions need time to make their own choices and to work through their grief in their own way, to talk or be silent as they wish. And they need some place to go where they can let their feelings explode, cry, scream, punch the furniture if need be, without restriction. The china-smashing stalls to be found on fairgrounds are fine for this purpose! On the other hand, some will find it difficult to give free rein to this necessary ventilation of feeling:

> Adults in their own grief, however loving, forget that children, especially older children, have understanding but no social behaviour to deal with the situation and need to be drawn out.

We need to consider how to provide talking situations and a climate in which the child feels free to express any of his feelings; he needs plenty of opportunities, without feeling pressurised, to talk about his memories, even perhaps some negative incident from the past:

> I never discouraged the children from talking about Mummy, nor even (on rare occasions) from grumbling that things would have been better if Mummy had been here. I am not one for having hard and fast rules for bringing up children, but I do believe that any taboo of that sort would have been disastrous.

Books, photographs and paints produce good talking opportunities, as do modelling and play with dolls or other toys. Give freedom for feelings to be expressed through acting out, art, music or sport. Children find relief for their grief both in tears and in physical activity, but there are other feelings, sometimes tangled and complicated, that can only find resolution through the filtering of language:

> Having had to console a child bereaved and one facing possible bereavement, the only thing that seemed helpful was to allow them to talk out their worst feelings, fears, anger without trying to stop the flow. Repression of these at this time is bad, I feel sure.

In trouble, children take their cue from watching how the adults around them react. They need to know that it is OK to pour out their feelings, and if they see those close to them doing so, they will more readily talk or weep or give way to their sorrow, which is of course just what they need to do. This applies not only to personal sorrows but also to the large-scale tragedies of which we have seen so many. From Enniskillen the Rev. Tom Magowan wrote:

> The courageous Christian witness has been a great help to the children both in Enniskillen and beyond. Thousands of letters have come from all over the world, some from schools or colleges and individual children who have been helped and encouraged by the way the relatives responded to the tragedy. We have found the children in the primary schools greatly impressed by the Christian courage shown and we believe that it will be a great help for them in coming to terms with bereavement in their own lives in the future.

Inclusion: a sense of belonging

There is a deep instinct in all of us to belong to the tribe, the family, to a bonded group. This sense of belonging is symbolised by parenthood, and when a father or mother dies something irretrievable is broken and lost. There is a breach in the walls: we cannot restore the person but we can gather together in our sorrow and show that we belong together. Children must be included in all such gatherings, never left out by accident or design, and made part of everything that is happening or that is planned to happen.

The funeral is a powerful visual expression of family unity, and the value of the occasion is now recognised. It provides:

- an opportunity to say a proper goodbye. Children feel a need for things to be done properly, for there to be a fitting end, a sense of completeness.

- an occasion when grief can be freely expressed, yet it is contained, shaped and ratified by the ritual.

- a real experience, far removed from the celluloid death of which children see too much on the screen. For some children this real experience provides the definitive evidence of the reality of their loss, making mourning possible.

- a time when there is a gathering together in sorrow, and the family draws close, so that help can be seen to be available.

- an affirmation of the child's selfhood as an integral part of the familial unit with a right to a place in the common front.

Children should be brought into any discussion and allowed to contribute their ideas. They can choose favourite hymns and prayers or passages from their own cultural rites. They can make their own posy of flowers or plant a rose:

When we used to visit my husband's grave I told them it was Daddy's memorial garden.

Myra Chave-Jones, who counsels adults suffering from neuroses stemming from childhood bereavement, supports the view that even little children should be allowed to attend, accompanied by a hand-holding, close adult. But the child's wishes should be consulted:

I am glad I was given the opportunity to see Dad's body in the coffin. My nine-year-old brother and I were both given this opportunity. I am glad that I said 'yes' and my brother is glad that he said 'no'. I am thankful that I was brought up in a culture (the north-east of Scotland) where death was not hidden away but was an event that everyone could share in. Visiting the bereaved, seeing the body (if we wanted to), attending the funeral were all open to children as well as adults.

Research now suggests that it is also wise to encourage children to touch the body. Such a decision would have to depend on particular circumstances – the feelings of the family, the child's wishes and perhaps professional advice. Anne Lingley has seen the positive outcome of this in her work as head of a hospice:

> I have personal experience of a five-year-old child who was present at the death of his three-year-old sister and who then very gently helped me wash and dress her, cut a lock of her hair and cuddle her in an unhurried and very natural way. He was completely unfrightened by the experience and it is a good and very positive memory for me.
>
> I would say that children should be encouraged to take part in such rituals if they *want* to.

Where a teacher or pupil from school has died, all those who had a relationship with that person should be given the choice of attending the funeral, where practical considerations allow.

> This frequently happens now, or else there is a special school occasion, but not many years ago, when it was the practice to exclude children, without exception they resented not being allowed to go to the funeral.

Understanding and comfort

Bereaved children need special care: what we do at this time may make a difference to their whole future life. The poignancy of their plight lies in the fact that the one they would normally turn to is the one who has gone. The one who warmed the chilled hands, who quelled the nightmare, raised up the failed examinee is now needed to help the child through her loss – needed in vain. Whoever breaks the news or stands in for the lost parent must have a regard for all the child's needs, emotional as well as physical: bodily comfort at such a time sends a message of reassurance and well-being.

A young teenager trying to take on adult responsibilities became lazy and very depressed:

He would sleep during the day and walk the streets and countryside at night. He was dismissed from one job for being late for work. His insomnia became a serious problem. A visit to the doctor was unhelpful, but a large jar of Horlicks and new flannelette sheets had some good effect.

Remember that adolescents are characteristically hard to rouse in the mornings (and bereavement makes people tired and shivery), that they may be struggling with exam pressure and that their heavy loss may make life hard to face. The situation is demanding for the lone parent who has to meet the daily necessities of life while at the same time keeping an eye on the children's welfare and state of mind. Even without the use of words a small child may reveal to a sensitive parent watching her play that something is troubling her. She might be worried that her naughtiness was the real cause of the death and could be helped by a simple explanation of what really happened. She could be told that being cross with someone cannot make them ill, or that the illness was too bad for the doctors to be able to cure it.

Practical ways of helping must vary according to age, personality and circumstances; for example:

I bought my nine-year-old a kitten, which she tended and looked after and was totally responsible for. I filled the house with friends of all ages. She joined an evangelical church, the members of which took a great interest in her. She joined the Girl Guides. She wept for the first three months every night and then never mentioned her father again. I think being kept busy, active, outward, helped too.

There is a great need for physical warmth and contact and for an outpouring of the healing power of love. Children need someone to hold them tight and cuddle them like a baby, while an adult may find comfort and healing through counselling and spiritual help.

It is never too late to mourn. People who in childhood were denied a place in family mourning have been helped many years later by participating in a retrospective funeral service.

Good management relies heavily on providing the right conditions for self-healing and this will depend on the quality of the whole system of support that the bereaved child can draw on.

POINTS TO REMEMBER

THE NEEDS OF A BEREAVED CHILD

- Openness: reliable information and truthful answers

- Freedom of expression: space

- DO tell the truth about what has happened – though not necessarily in detail or all at once

- DON'T avoid the subject or give inaccurate information

- DO answer questions as they are asked

- DON'T give gratuitous information the child may not be ready for

- DO encourage the child to weep and talk – but in her own time

- DON'T pressurise the child

- DO give plenty of scope for free ventilation of feeling in a variety of ways

- DON'T stop talking when the child comes into the room

- DO minimise changes – avoid moving if possible

- DON'T repress unusual expressions of grief

- DO provide books, writing and drawing materials and plenty of opportunity for physical activities

- DO be honest with your own feelings

- DON'T pretend to a cheerfulness you do not feel

- Inclusion: a sense of belonging

- Understanding and comfort

- DO encourage the child to attend the funeral accompanied by a significant adult

- DON'T let her feel ignored or overlooked

- DO be sensitive to individual needs

- DON'T expect all children to behave in the same way

6

Facing the future:
the needs of the growing child

. . . called upon to uphold with her childish might the broken
end of the arch.

In *The Rainbow* D. H. Lawrence pictures the little girl Anna,
whose father has died, as feeling responsible for her widowed
mother. It is often true that even little children try to take on
responsibility for comforting their parent. Children will try to
fill the empty place, even to the extent of forgoing marriage
themselves when they grow up. Each child has inner resources of
personality and coping ability, but these should not be stretched
to the limit. They should not have the added burden of anxiety
about a lonely parent. The first concern of those caring for the
child must be to support the surviving parent.

The main issues that have to be considered are:

- Care

- Modelling

- A framework of discipline

- Restoring self-esteem and rebuilding trust

Care

Children's nurturing needs change as they grow into adolescence, so that the ways in which we can support the lone parent

will change too. Over the years there will be many different needs, and help for coping with these will have to be drawn from the immediate family circle and beyond: from neighbours and friends; from school and teachers; from professionals such as the GP and pastor or rabbi; and sometimes from the community as a whole, including social workers, health visitors and police.

Home fires

Keeping the home base in working order is crucial for the sake of the children.

> The first thing I asked Mum was could we keep Skippy and Shadow, our cat and dog, and could we keep our house, and she said 'Sure'.[1]

Restoring a shattered sense of security means seeing that some things can stay the same, helping Mum to say 'Sure' to such questions. It needs both sensitivity and imagination to visualise the situation in a bereaved home:

> It is funny how comparatively small things can become large in certain circumstances. I rather expected that some of the church people might have invited us for Sunday lunch, and they didn't. It would be too much to say I was hurt by this – after all, they were marvellous in so many ways. But until I was used to it I did find getting Sunday lunch organised (with Timmy in nappies at that time) a bit much.

Caring for the home base means, if possible, finding relatives, neighbours or else paid help to undertake the practical chores and free the parent from frustrating domestic worries. He can then work through his own grief unhindered, enter into the children's sorrow and keep the family together.

Caring for the children will depend upon their age. A very young baby, who is as yet of course unaware of his own identity, is likely to adjust to the loss of his mother without too much trauma if another caretaker can be found who will be constant, warm and caring, who will study his needs, maintain his accustomed routine and surround him with love. It is best if he can be kept in his own home and cared for by the one person.

Help must be consistent, regular and reliable: a hard-pressed pastor from Blaenavon wrote:

> The problem of baby-sitting was less than it might have been. I tried to arrange regular people for the nights when I was regularly out, and work from a small number of people for other occasions ... I'm sure it was better for the children. Fortunately I was already reasonably domesticated so that I wasn't doing many things that I hadn't done before, just having full responsibility for them all. We already had a lady helping with the cleaning from when Gill was teaching.

Local head teachers may be prepared to stretch their usual commitments in a case of dire necessity:

> ... how helpful the local nursery was. We had booked Timmy to start the September after Gill's death ... but the head rang to say that now I was a one-parent family he could start as soon as he was three, although this meant they had to cope with his nappies.

Pre-school children who have been bereaved, especially of Mummy, may understandably take longer to settle into playgroup or nursery school, and having had one loss may show a tendency to hang on possessively to the toys they play with and to need more attention. They should be given plenty of cuddling time on the teacher's lap until they seem ready to take an interest in what is going on and join in with the other children.

Guidelines for helping in the home:

- Good intentions are not enough: time is a major casualty in a bereaved household and arrangements, once made, cannot be changed without ample warning.

- It is no use offering help in the first flush of sympathy and finding after a few weeks that it cannot be maintained. Helpers' family holidays must give precedence to the needs of the bereaved family they are pledged to support.

- Offers of help must be specific: e.g. DAILY – cooking evening meals; getting lunch boxes ready for the morning; washing and ironing; OCCASIONAL – buttons and mending; fuses and washers; mowing the lawn; turning up curtain hems, etc. Keep to your own job – it is infuriating to turn up and find that someone else has already done it!

- Rotas for meeting children from school or having them in for tea must be infallible. In these hazardous times there are too many dangers. It does not contribute to security to go to school with a key round the neck or to go back to an empty house. Children should never be left in the house without an adult for the risk of fire or intruders.

Care of school-age children involves being adaptable to change – seeing them through the stresses of physical and emotional change, changes of friends, schools and perhaps circumstances. Although school moves at seven and eleven are routine, they may seem epoch-making in the inner world of a child whose need is for stability. On the eve of the Great Fun Day, Kit would have preferred his usual programme of project work. 'I don't want to go to school tomorrow. Everything's going to be different.' At the end of the summer term when David realised he would be losing his friends to a different class in the autumn, he cried all night.

At each new stage care means that general health, physical growth, eyes, teeth, emotional development, moods and perhaps incipient rebellious feelings must be taken into account, and school progress reassessed. 'Is she working too hard?' 'Is he being bullied?' 'Are they following their natural aptitudes in subject choices?' As they move towards major exams someone must see that they are getting a balanced diet (actually *eating* the packed lunch) and that the child who puts everything into life is combating nervous exhaustion by getting enough sleep.

It is desperately discouraging for a child who has no one to take an interest in his school activities and achievements. Someone must be found to turn up in a parent's place on Open Day and Sports Day, to see him win the high jump or play the cello or admire her Viola in *Twelfth Night*. Someone must take note of these encouraging triumphs, follow academic progress and discuss career prospects or disruptive behaviour. Whoever has the overall responsibility must see that the worlds of home and school do not grow so far apart that what is happening in one place is not known in another.

Care becomes more problematical as children reach the teen years and begin to go their own way. It's hard for a lone mother to know where to draw boundaries and how to maintain the hours and regime that Dad would have held. If she makes a fuss when they arrive home in the early hours, they may in future opt to stay overnight at a friend's house – and she loses the connection.

At this age children themselves have pressures to contend with – zits, teeth braces, relationships, hormonal and emotional pressures and simply growing too fast. We should avoid adding to these by nagging unduly about exam results, having too high expectations or idealising the deceased parent beyond hope of emulating. Better to try and become interested in their world, their sport, their music, to buy them some Clearskin and favourite body spray, and keep a sense of humour. This stage does not last for ever! But now is the time to enlist help from the support system.

Modelling

Throughout their growing years children are engaged on the task of establishing who they are and what their role in life is to be.

They will find patterns from stage, screen and sport, from fiction and from among those they admire in their circle of relatives, teachers and friends. Parents are the most important of all because the modelling is instinctive rather than intentional. Small children will copy whatever the parent present is doing – watering the garden, making a cake – but gradually they begin to take on the behaviour patterns of the same-sex parent. A clear view of sex roles is important to a child discovering his or her own self, and the loss of such a model when a parent dies may swing the balance towards depression or deviant orientation. In bringing up children there are many things that have to be passed on by instruction, but values and qualities such as courage, integrity, considerateness and truthfulness are largely modelled. Many of these precious traits might be lost when a parent dies, but they do not need to be if the memory is kept alive.

The memory model

I believe that drawing attention to the things I admired in him – honesty, sympathy, consideration for other people, a sense of humour, high spirits, a gentle voice, and so on – will help them more than if I never mentioned him . . . of course they knew he was no plaster saint. They can still remember his human shortcomings themselves: the fuss he made about going to the dentist, for instance, and the holes he made in the blanket from smoking in bed.[2]

Be careful to keep the memory a rounded and realistic one, not only because it is true, but also because a too highly idealised one may give the children an impossible goal to aim for, and prove a discouragement rather than a spur.

Keeping a realistic memory alive, 'warts and all', can make a continuing support for someone trying to bring up a family on their own. One widow found that people would avoid bringing her husband into the conversation for fear of reopening the wound, but there was nothing she liked better than hearing about him:

I made a point of keeping him present. Whenever a decision had to be made, whether it was over the family or the job I had to take, I now asked myself, 'What would he have done?' and the answer was immediately obvious. This thought must have crept into my conversation with the children. They also asked me what he would have done. When the little ones started school, they went off conscious of their father and as proud of him as if he had driven them himself in the car, as the other fathers drove their daughters. Four years have passed and my husband's influence on the family is as strong as ever.[3]

It sometimes happens that when someone dies the survivor cannot bear the pain of remembering and gets rid of clothes and possessions as fast as possible. Photos are hidden away and belongings sent to a charity shop. However, the effect of this precipitate action can bring about an overwhelming sense of guilt and remorse and a reaction of returning memories which will then rekindle the pain in a vicious circle of conflicting emotions. Where children are concerned it is a great mistake to try to shut the door to memories. The hiding of belongings and the removal of photos makes a strong negative statement:

> Dad admits now that the death was not handled well for John and me. Her photo was taken off the wall and my brother stood looking at the empty gap and said: 'My mummy used to be there.'

If there are children it is important that there should be reminders of the loved parent about the house and memories kept alive. A photo by the bedside is like a goodnight prayer. A rose tree planted, a grave or a corner of the garden kept special, makes a focus for memory in a way that may answer a need for even a very young child. At three years old, whenever life became too bewildering for Mary, she would ask someone to take her to visit her baby brother's grave. She did not know his body was there, but it was a way of remembering. The grave was decorated with wild roses and honeysuckle.

Keepsakes also offer comfort to a sad heart. Many years after her brother died Ann found a need to treasure something of his:

> I had some of his possessions and began looking for others. I had, for example, a New Testament belonging to him and this became a very important possession. One day one of my classmates wrote or drew something on one of the pages and I remember being very angry and unreasonably upset.

Six years after her father fell from his bike under a bus, Jenny kept her father's memory alive with one of his socks:

> Jenny had a sock puppet she had made two weeks ago and told me proudly that it was 'Daddy's sock'. She has taken possession of 'Daddy's bath towel' and when I am super-vising bath-time and ask 'Whose towel belongs to who?' she always informs me that she has 'Daddy's towel'.

The SAS honour their dead with a plaque in the local parish church of St Martin's, Hereford, and memorial vases with individually chosen stone-engraved messages from each of the bereaved families. The vases are not just places for flowers but a setting where the widows and their families can remember the men whose bodies were never recovered. After the Falklands War the Government arranged for widows to visit the Islands so they could show their children where their fathers had died. The children had proudly shown their friends photographs of the father they would always remember as a hero.

The day before June left for the Falklands she walked to the village churchyard to lay spring flowers on the grey Cornish granite memorial to a man who was buried in the South Atlantic. Etched on the plaque were the words: 'Andrew Peter Evans 1949–1982. He lived and died bravely that others might live freely.'[4]

Maybe we have forgotten that during the Second World War

many thousands of mothers had to bring up a family on their own while Dad was away fighting and perhaps never returned. Those mothers refused to allow their husbands' sacrifice to count for nothing, their lives and influence to be lost to the children. Memories can make powerful models. Mothers and fathers who have died are still mums and dads, still part of the children's lives, patterns for their future.

A framework of discipline

All youngsters need to know that life is not a chaotic confusion and that a balance must be struck between the individual and the reasonable demands of society. And this becomes imperative when the support and authority of a parent have been lost and grief sweeps away customary respect for norms of behaviour. In these circumstances 'discipline' means responding to a need for boundaries. Bereavement makes us question the control we have over our lives. Some people may feel that:

> There's a divinity that shapes our ends,
> Rough-hew them how we will.
> (*Hamlet* V:ii:10)

It brings changes to which we must adapt and anxieties that may cause us to lose a sense of perspective. For the young this may mean panic attacks, a loss of control and a fear of chaos. When the security of family life has been shattered, patterns and structures become very desirable.

It is difficult not to over-react to a boy who becomes ungovernable, either to overwhelm him with futile sympathy or to hand out some possibly inappropriate punishment. Neither is likely to be productive. It is better to take time when there is no immediate crisis to try to agree calmly about what might be acceptable limits and how to avoid overstepping them.

Organisations such as Scouts and Guides are helpful in building a sense of order and purpose into the lives of the young by channelling their energies into meaningful activities, providing an escape valve for overwrought emotion. They also provide the acceptable voice of lost authority, which can be reflected in the home as order and stability are restored.

One mother found that taking a firm line was effective:

> I was unable to maintain a high level of discipline when it was needed. Roy did not cope with school work. He left after completing only one year in the sixth form. His behaviour deteriorated so much during 1983 that I gave him an ultimatum: change your behaviour or get out. And I meant it! He changed – quite dramatically too! Since starting at the Polytechnic in October 1983 he has become quite friendly and co-operative. He has also had time to sit and think and to think about his dad. At last he has been able to grieve: painful but beneficial.

But confrontation is best avoided by entering into the child's tough situation, by keeping in mind his deeply wounded psyche and by being always first to seek forgiveness and reconciliation. He needs building up, not slapping down: children learn better from approval and encouragement than from blame or criticism.

The real reason why children should wish to conform is because they love their parents, and this applies equally whether there is one parent or two.

Self-esteem and trust

Self-esteem is one of the major casualties of bereavement. A child who has both parents has a balancing measure for building his identity. When one of them dies the balance is lost, the needle swings and he no longer knows who he is or where he is going. The fact that there is no longer the same mutual authority as a defence against undue peer pressure can be a fearful source of insecurity. When his friends arrive for parents' meetings with both parents and he has only one he feels that he has lost status.

Restoring a sense of self-worth must be made a high priority by those concerned. It is an essential attribute for a successful adult life, and steps to its revival begin with reassurance, restoring the sense of security and safety which bolster trust.

- Bereaved children need the reassurance that their needs will continue to be met, that they are safe: that the material and emotional bases of their life will not be lost as well.

- They need respect. Their ideas should have serious consideration and their wishes about plans for the future should be given due weight.

- They need to be listened to. This means that they may need to be allowed to ask the same questions over and over again: 'My brother's elder child, aged seven, died, and I think the greatest help to the younger (two years younger) was just talking – finding the right medium in which the child can express her feelings.' No one can 'talk' unless they feel that they are being listened to and heard, but listening properly is not easy. Listening is an art.

- They need to be set free from guilt and helped to resolve their fear and anger. A small child who is blaming himself for the death may be helped by a simple explanation of the real cause, but older children may have real anxieties and burdens of conscience. They should be given the opportunity of talking with a counsellor or pastor or spiritual adviser from their own background.

- They need to be accepted as normal responsible persons, neither shunned nor overburdened with sympathy, and to take their place in the school in line with the usual behavioural codes, not suddenly made a 'special case' with special privileges.

- They need opportunities to create. Creativity is a means of expressing personality and of communicating feelings at times when those feelings lie too deep for words. It is a gift through which young people can find healing for their emotional wounds. All children have a gift of their own, and self-esteem grows by having that gift nurtured and encouraged. In long years of teaching I have never come across a child who has no special personal gift – for example, it may be gifts of caring and helping and of serving others.

- They need praise. Find what he or she is good at and provide opportunities to excel, not only in sport and practical matters, but in the even more rewarding moral qualities. Recognise every character trait and personal victory with praise.

- They need the commitment of an adult. They need to know that someone loves them unconditionally and come what may. This is an essential element in self-esteem. This is what we look for in our parents. When a child's self-esteem has been shattered by the loss or defection of a parent, we need to express the high value we place on him by our love and comforting.[5]

Darren was always in trouble. He had a very unsettled background and was living with foster parents. One day he was sent to the head teacher for punishment because of some particularly obnoxious misdemeanour. She knew he was very disturbed and aggressive. 'Why do you do these things?' she asked. He hung his head. 'I haven't got a real mummy and daddy,' he said. 'Nobody cares about me.'

'I do', said the head teacher. 'I care.'

In the USA they have an organisation called Big Brothers, through which men and women give the sort of dedication needed to children who have lost a parent by death or divorce. Links are made with the children through guidance counsellors.

My mother died in September and I got my new Big Sister in October . . . We see each other every weekend and we do things like go to movies and go ice-skating. And we go out to eat a lot. But the best thing we do is just talk. Meeting Mary is about the most wonderful thing that ever happened to me.[6]

The next chapter contains an outline of some sources of help.

POINTS TO REMEMBER

THE NEEDS OF THE BEREAVED CHILD

FACING THE FUTURE
The main issues to be considered are:

- CARE

- MODELLING

- A FRAMEWORK OF DISCIPLINE

- RESTORING SELF-ESTEEM AND REBUILDING TRUST

DO support and comfort the surviving parent
DO try to maintain the established ways of the home
DO be realistic in offering help and reliable in keeping to agreed rotas, shifts and workloads
DO take an interest in the children's school activities and successes
DO provide back-up for children pressured by their peers
DO help to keep a rounded and realistic memory of the dead parent alive, but without idealising him or her
DON'T be afraid to talk about him or her
DON'T remove all photographs, belongings and reminders
DO provide firm and reasonable behavioural codes
DON'T over-react to exhibitions of temper or rebellious behaviour
DO try to maintain an equable atmosphere in the home and establish a climate of reassurance and trust
DO give ample praise and encouragement, opportunities for creativity, companionship and commitment

---

7

A tree of healing: sources of support

Those who are loved will often survive deprivation and catastrophe beyond belief.

Support from the church and community has been good. We are a close-knit community and caring is made easier because of the size of the town of Enniskillen.

This chapter is not intended to give an exhaustive list of sources but to offer examples of many different ways in which people in various walks of life have been able to help restore a good quality of life for children who have been damaged by the loss of a parent.

In the event of need people will look first to the professionals, the GP, health visitors and social workers through whom they will be able to gain referral, if need be, to psychiatrists and Child Guidance clinics. But there may not be a need for specialist help, and children's lives are set within many different contexts, all of which may contribute to the healing process.

No one can tell who may be the person called upon to step in at some critical moment and give the child the comfort and understanding she needs. It may be the kind lady at the corner shop or the caretaker in the local school; it may be a prison officer or the night porter in the Accident and Emergency Department of a hospital; it may be a barmaid in a bombed Irish pub. It may be you.

A child's distraught grief leaves adults floundering, and the community as a whole needs to be aware of the seriousness of childhood bereavement and be prepared to take on a responsibility for children at a crisis point in their lives.

Community spirit takes over

I contacted the local social services, the police, the Juvenile Liaison Bureau, the NSPCC, the church and anyone else that would listen to me, but help was not available. The children were either too old or I didn't live in the right neighbourhood or I hadn't battered them.

It is ten years since the tragic sinking of the *Derbyshire*, when Marion Bayliss wrote to me about her inability to find help for her bereaved children. Since then the situation throughout the country has changed. This is due very largely to the work of Dr Dora Black, to the growth of the CRUSE organisation, to a growing awareness of the problems of bereaved children which have been aired on the media and to the number of major disasters that have thrown us, as a nation, into mourning.

Wherever there have been large-scale disasters there have been support groups set up as a matter of course – for the *Herald of Free Enterprise*, the Locherbie air crash, the massacre in Tasmania and for Dunblane, to mention a few – and as a general rule the CRUSE organisation has inspired the training and provided the back-up. A church-based helper from Surrey wrote:

I am on the Pastoral Team of our Church, and as I am a CRUSE counsellor the minister asks me to visit if there is a need. I get all my back-up and support from CRUSE.

From Portsmouth one member of a church's support group wrote about the legacy of the Falklands War, which hit the children of that particular corner of England very hard:

You are right in thinking the Falklands War affected people down here, it certainly did. Everyone knew someone who was involved . . . Many teachers had children whose fathers were involved. The Naval Family Welfare people sent fifteen people to us to be trained as they felt themselves to be inadequate . . . I am sure your findings will reveal that children are not catered for adequately.

Dr Black's research into the effects of family-based intervention has found her methods helpful in enabling children to grieve and express their sorrow, and in mitigating short-term distress, such as depression, learning difficulties and behavioural problems. It is beneficial to children and teenagers if a social worker or other professional can meet with the whole family and enable them to mourn together. Yet despite this evidence, after the Bradford fire Michael Stewart did not find it easy to arrange such seminars because of the anxiety of the parents.

Furthering these aims is helped if the children are given the support of a tightly knit community.

A close-knit community

We have looked at possible unhappy results of childhood bereavement and at factors that can cause problems, but there are also many examples where tragedy seems to have been successfully negotiated. What was good about the management of the situation?

Nichola and Timmy lost their mother when Nichola was eight and Timmy three . . . the valley communities in South Wales are well known for their community spirit, and Blaenavon is said by some impartial observers to be perhaps the best of them all in that respect. I certainly felt that there was an abundance of goodwill, both within and outside the churches, which was waiting to be expressed in any form I might wish.

Looking back six years after their mother's death, Nichola's and Timmy's father wrote:

I have little doubt from things that are said that folk here would say we had coped well.

Enniskillen is a small town where many of the families are not only close as neighbours, but also interrelated. Everyone had someone who was killed, injured or traumatised by the IRA bomb:

Some families have been experiencing delayed shock, with children suffering from nightmares and becoming listless. Some who at the time were coping well are now, several months afterwards, experiencing difficulty in sleeping at nights and depressed. . . Nearly all have resumed normal occupations and daily routine. The bereaved families are coping very well, some better than others. The fact that they all had fairly close church connections has been a tremendous help.

The community spirit of the South Wales valleys and of the little town of Enniskillen obviously plays a major role in creating a protective frame of mind. Most residents are part of an extended family. Other factors that were mentioned from Enniskillen were:

- Relief from anxieties about money

- The value of the CRUSE seminars

- Co-operation with other support groups from major disasters

- Keeping closely in touch with the bereaved families

The Appeal Fund has relieved anxiety about financial problems and immediate bills have been met by the Fund . . . the Social Services and the Local Education Authority have held several seminars for teachers, social workers and ministers. These have been well attended and proved useful. The CRUSE organisation has also been helping with several seminars for those dealing with the families and this has been most useful. The Appeal Fund sought the help of those who coped with the

Bradford, Hungerford and ferry disasters. The co-operation between medical staff and ministers was excellent both at the time of the incident and since. They have certainly been brought closer together through their support of each other at that time. The fact that the families involved are church-going meant that the ministers have been able to keep in very close touch with each family on a regular basis of pastoral visitation.

A constructive response

Death through war and violence brings complex emotions in addition to the expected anger which is a customary phase of bereavement. In particular, it brings desire for revenge. Unless this desire is satisfied the wound in the heart is deepened by frustration and bitterness. This is an underlying cause of the constant cycle of wars and civil strife that has plagued our century, not only in Northern Ireland, but worldwide.

This is what makes the response of the little town of Enniskillen so impressive, for it would appear that they have found a balm which can not only heal the wound but halt the cycle:

> The children and the community were stunned by the event and outraged that this could happen on an occasion like a Remembrance Day Sunday wreath-laying. There was also a great deal of anger felt against those who planted the bomb. This could have resulted in a massive retaliation by the paramilitary groups, which was only prevented by the Christian response of the bereaved, especially the words of forgiveness and plea for no retaliation by Mr Gordon Wilson, whose daughter was killed and whose reaction made such an impression all over the world.

The potential of the local church

It is possible to underestimate the extent and quality of support given by ministers of every denomination in the course of their normal duties. Letters and case histories speak gratefully of the hours and effort spent on their behalf by over-stretched pastors and lay workers, in spiritual and practical matters.

> With the help of a Methodist minister I was able to sort myself out.

> A couple from the local Catholic church called. They were part of an organisation that helped people in trouble. They even got hold of a second-hand washing machine for me. I was very lonely and desperately needed someone to talk to.

> We are Anglicans and also belong to a small ecumenical group in our village. This group have been a marvellous support and have shared everything with us, particularly Tom's last weeks at home.

Their ministry to bereaved children will operate through established friendship in various ways, such as open homes where bereaved children are invited in on a regular basis; shared holidays; outings and sports. In the USA, 'Big Brothers' and 'Big Sisters' are arranged through the local church. It is important to keep special anniversaries. Churches may offer training in listening skills of youth leaders.

The personal touch

Teenagers appreciate receiving cards and letters personally rather than as one of the family, and some may like a chance to talk privately. Little individual kindnesses mean much. Pauline lost her mother at 13:

> I had had the day off school and was bewildered on answering the doorbell to see a school friend handing me a great bunch of flowers. I stammered that they were too late, but she said they were for *me*. I could hardly believe her kindness.

The Rev. Sandy Gunn offers these guidelines for conduct of funerals where children are involved:

Children should be involved at the time of the trouble with everything being explained . . . care should be taken to ensure that the child is not swamped by a lot of adults and has an opportunity to ask questions naturally . . . it can be helpful for youngsters to be involved in the actual preparation of a funeral service so that they can feel involved when 'their bit' is included . . . friends, not just the minister, need to be involved in follow-up.

An understanding of the spiritual, psychological and practical needs of the bereaved is of the first importance for those training for pastoral responsibilities. This is generally recognised as far as adults are concerned, but the needs of children are less well served. It is reassuring to see the full treatment that this is given in the pastoral counselling course at Oak Hill Theological College and this may be an indication of the way things are going. In addition to their general courses, Oak Hill College provides one specifically related to the needs of children, which is available not only to those training for the ordained ministry, but also to most other students. It covers a child's understanding of death, possible reaction to loss, grieving behaviour, advice on how to talk to a child about a death and how to help.

The GP

It is self-evident that GPs must hold a key role in situations of family tragedy. Having probably attended the person who has died, the GP may well be fully in possession of all the circumstances and relationships. They may have a role in the lives of the bereaved children, having to identify the nature of symptoms such as sleeping and eating disorders, deciding whether they are purely physical or have some deeper cause that may need referral to Child Guidance. They may support family morale and perhaps offer evidence where a disturbed youngster has had a brush with the law:

We have a very supportive GP, who was constantly in and out of our house, just as a support, not to offer medical help.

and

Our doctors' practice here is a group, but the leading one is a Pakistani, a Muslim, who took a great interest in Timmy because his natural parents were Pakistanis and they had the same last name. He went out of his way to be helpful, inviting me to his home and commenting that if he were in this situation he would shut himself away with the Holy Koran for some days! It was he who made the suggestion of getting a regular baby-sitter for the nights when I was regularly out – a simple suggestion but one which hadn't occurred to me at the time and was a great boon. He also reminded me that he and his colleagues were always available.

The health visitor

One letter says it all:

The function of the health visitor is to promote the maximum state of health of the child, the family and the community in all dimensions – including emotional well-being. Bereavement care is surely a part of this function.

In recent months my colleagues and I have talked to children about death, the death of particular people, taken them to funerals, to view lately deceased relatives, and continued to support them and their families in an ongoing and long-term programme.

One autumn day I was to be found rooting through leaves looking for conkers, with which to explain to a little boy that his mummy's poor sick body had died, like the shell of the chestnut, but the real person was living like the shiny conker.

This sort of care is vital when the adults around them are struggling with their own grief, and unable to relate to that of the children. Every child in this country has a health visitor – in fact the recent 'Children's Charter' states that a health visitor should visit every baby between ten and fourteen days of age, and every under-five within five working days of registration on a GP's list, in order to make initial contact. While I am well aware that there are gaps in the service for a variety of reasons, the principle is established.

A health visitor is well placed to help children in grief as she (or he) may well be a known visitor to the family. This has certainly been the case in several situations in which my colleagues in neighbouring practices and I myself have been involved.

I find that children ask me the questions they are afraid to present to their parents, for fear of upsetting them, and use me to reflect on things they cannot understand. They also say things they sense would upset already distressed parents.

This may not be the case in every family, but certainly health visitors should be seen as a resource to bereaved children, as to any other family need.

At times the skills needed are more specific, and in my experience I have been able to see this and refer to a Child Guidance team or psychologist for further help and counsel.[1]

Prison and prison officers

When fathers are arrested and taken off to prison, mothers are left in a state of shock. The pain and shame blight the whole family and affect the children's progress at school. The loss of the father comprises a devastating form of bereavement:

We had only recently moved to the area, so the neighbours didn't know much about us. So when he went to prison a full account of his crime, vividly described, took up the whole front page of the local paper. The village newsagent advertised the article on a board outside his shop. We were all judged as guilty and ostracised. The eldest boy had a terrible time at school as did the others. Children can be very cruel, aided and abetted by parents who don't want criminals living on their doorstep. The whole episode was a devastating experience. The younger two did suffer with their education – definitely they didn't achieve and the youngest still has reading problems. Angela has needed a lot of emotional healing and Billy really needs it too. He had a lot of fights at school. When the judge passed sentence on my husband he passed sentence on the whole family. I think the greatest problem at this time was being so short of money, and loneliness – cut off from society and feeling worthless.

However, there are many compassionate officers who have concern for the plight of mothers and children, and a growing spirit of sensitivity is transforming the service.

Bob started his sentence at Cardiff. While he was there I became very good friends with his Probation Officer; she was able to help us in many situations after . . . she helped us get travelling expenses so that things could be made a little easier when we went to see Bob . . . the Chaplain would very often phone and sometimes let Bob speak to us . . . in fact we've become very friendly with him. In all the prisons Bob was in they had play areas for the children, and in one they were supervised.

The police and their changing role

We are used to thinking of the police primarily as apprehending criminals, but their role is becoming increasingly one of supporting the victims, with a particular regard for the young. In an interview Detective Inspector Mick Mann told me how they provide role models, discipline and guidance for young offenders and support for lone mothers. He finds the situation is more difficult when it is the father who is lost because the children miss the authority figure in the family. It's their dad that troubled boys need. They want to follow their father.

Mick Mann recalled instances where he has been able to step into the place of a missing father and felt that his influence played a part in the healing process. For instance, a girl ('totally beside herself') whose husband had committed suicide was left with a ten-year-old son who reacted to the tragedy by extreme swings of mood, from happy-go-lucky to criminal damage, breaking windows of parked cars. There is a limit to what police can do when the offenders are under age, Mick pointed out. In this case he could only support the mother, for he did not want the boy to regard him as the big stick. But the wealth of experience police officers gain gives them depth of understanding. He was able to talk with the boy and make a relationship so that within the space of a year the delinquent behaviour had stopped.

Breaking the news – It often falls to the lot of the police to have to break the news of some terrible tragedy to a family. Every officer must be prepared at a young age to deal with such situations. In breaking news they are careful not to go straight to the stricken home, but to try and find another family member or neighbour to support the widow and to make sure that children are not left on their own.

Support and protection – It is evident that much forethought goes into police guidelines for dealing with tragic situations, especially with regard to healing the wounds of the young. They are able to intervene in situations where there are arguments between paternal and maternal relatives about where children should live or disputes over children's possessions.

> We have seen examples of very good practice where all these pitfalls have been avoided and the police have enabled brothers and sisters to be together in privacy, have cared for them, kept them warm (fear and anxiety make people cold and shivery) talked to them about what was happening and stayed on duty while relatives were found.[2]

The hospice movement

The first hospice for care of terminally ill children was Helen House in Oxford, but there are now about eight in the country, whose mission consists not only in caring for sick children, many terminally ill, but also in providing for their needs in the context of the whole family.

Family-centred care means supporting the whole family, empowering the parents to care for their child and at the same time keeping in view the needs of the other children. Siblings of children facing death have a very difficult time. It is not only a question of the approaching bereavement; sometimes it may be a matter of a long-term congenital ailment, which means the whole family may be suffering from grief for years before the child dies.

Again, the needs of siblings will not only be for bereavement counselling and the healing of grief, but for coping with feelings of jealousy and deprivation. 'Why is this brother special? Why is he never, as I am, punished for his outbursts of temper?' The well sibling may not realise how short a time is left for the parents to enjoy their dying child, and may resent the fact that she is punished for faults unregarded in her ailing brother, or that her immediate needs often seem to be overlooked.

The whole family life is disrupted: even an ordinary seaside holiday may be beyond their hopes. This kind of deprivation of the normal expectations of childhood can make younger children especially very aggressive and they may work out their frustration and grief in outbursts of anger. Then when the sibling dies they are plagued by insecurity and fear, guilt-ridden about things they wish they had not said and done. Their need is to be able to talk about and share their situation with other children who are similarly placed. The hospice at Quidenham in Suffolk, to take just one example, plans to provide more active sibling support – something special for them to give them some personal attention and counteract their feeling of being 'outsiders'. The well children suffer a terrible blow in the loss of a normal child's life and expectations; in some the enduring legacy may even be a fear of marrying, in case their children inherit a fatal disease. There is a similar loss for the parents, who have looked forward to seeing their child grow up but must now face his death. Not only do they lose the child, but are faced with agonising years of pain and grief before he dies.

Family and neighbours – mature friends

The kind of help one might generally expect from family and neighbours has been outlined in the last chapter, but there are also particular ways in which the gap left by an absent father needs to be filled:

- Voice of authority – An uncle or man friend can provide the back-up in responsibility and leadership that children look for in a dad.

- Balance – He can provide a balance by seeing things from the boy's point of view, e.g. preventing an overprotective mother from following him with an umbrella on his newspaper round.

- Fatherly friend – Mature male friends can give a boy something he cannot otherwise get: a pattern of behaving like a dad for when he has children of his own:

  A great help to me in the years after Dad's death was the care and interest of other men. There were one or two particularly in our church's after-church get-together who played with me and let me sit on their knee. They never took the place of Dad – but they were good friends.

- Confidant – Mature friends can give the adolescent boy or girl who has lost the same-sex parent a confidant to whom they can talk about things that may trouble them, rather than relying on the advice of Agony Aunts in teenage magazines or on peer-group ideas that may get them into trouble.

Peer group – same-age friends

The advantage of having friends of the same age is that they look at life from a similar perspective, the viewpoint of their world, not an adult world. They are doing the same things in the same places and so do not have to make special moments to talk. Thoughts and feelings can be shared as they arise.

Some of them may well be in a similar situation to the bereaved child in having only one parent at home, and in sharing a great need to feel valued and accepted. One spin-off of so many broken homes is that these children no longer stand out like sore thumbs, are no longer so different from their peers. A mother of teenagers who lost their dad wrote:

Their various peer groups were mostly admirable and very supportive. Occasionally Roy's friends were unkind, but this was dealt with quite adequately by the school.

The companionship that friends of the same age can offer can be a significant factor in the healing process. Any teasing or ostracism at a time like this can delay the resolution of grief or turn an unhappy youngster to solvent abuse, for example, and the need for counselling. But in fact it is more likely that those with problems will help each other: 'I was interested, though, in the fact that Roy made friends with boys who also did not have a father.'

Alan, a disruptive boy from a problem home, palled up with a boy whose father had died and shouldered the responsibility of creating a good environment for him. Alan's difficulties began to fall away in his concern for the bereaved boy and in helping him; at the same time the boy who had lost his father benefited from his companionship.[3]

Children can be remarkably perceptive:

When Tom was dying some of his friends called regularly during his last weeks at home and sat with him. He was due to start at a new school and two of his classmates from the village called twice to tell him about the school. All the class wrote letters, although he had never met some of them. Since his death two of his friends call regularly to see us and one at boarding-school writes and telephones, which shows great sensitivity in a twelve-year-old boy.

Rainbows

The special place of peer support is recognised in Rainbows, an organisation founded in the USA a decade ago to help children through their grieving, on the principle that children can help each other. Children who have been bereaved by death, divorce or separation can talk through their feelings with other children who are in similar situations. They are helped to verbalise their thoughts by adults who are not counsellors but are trained in listening skills. Rainbows groups meet in places where children gather – schools, church halls, youth clubs – and use workbooks, story books, games and activities to form a structured programme designed to lead children gently through the grieving process and to support them in rebuilding their self-esteem.

School – an alternative world

The school should be a major source of support in offering routine, predictability and a different environment for a child who has had the world of home knocked from under his feet. It may be considered the child's first line of defence, the teachers his closest allies.

Schools must be prepared for the fact that some children will not be able to face returning to school following a bereavement; they may not feel equal to the task of learning and may either opt out or, if they do arrive, they may be a disturbing influence. Truancy and disruptive behaviour are both cries for help, expressing a longing for the security of an unbroken home. School life goes some way to supplying those needs, especially where teachers are alert to uncharacteristic behaviour and its reason. Punishment is not the answer, but while discipline must be maintained, it must be tempered by insight and understanding.

Safe haven

For some pupils school will offer a respite. At home the atmosphere may be charged with emotion; everything may be topsy turvy, perhaps with kindly people coming and going at odd hours but with little time to give them the real attention that they need. It may be reassuring to start the day with a schedule that is normal and familiar. Older children may find that the boundaries and timetables that were once so frustrating are now a source of relief, and the effort of having to think about something other than their personal grief may even be helpful. A gradual return to curriculum, work schedules and homework enables a child to return to normal school life without pressure. Creative activities in school such as dance, drama and music are channels of release for overwrought emotions and may go some way towards averting the dangers of inhibited grief.

Where a child has been witness to violent death, drawing, modelling and verbal communication may be means of enabling him to pin down his experience. Children exposed to horrific visual images suffer nightmares and recurrent flashbacks: creative activities in school may help to reduce these effects, and enable children to identify their own feelings. It is best if such children can be seen very soon after such an event by someone skilled in interviewing children, and monitored at intervals afterwards.

Bridge the gap

Sometimes there is a communication gap between children and parents. They may have reached an age when it is difficult to open their heart; or they may be afraid of burdening the parent with their own sorrow and reopening the parent's wound. A teacher who understands the boy or girl may be the best person to bridge this gap and establish communication between parent and child. He may actually have to break the news if both parents have been killed – he may be the closest person left.

A helpful function of the school is to provide reliable facts and lines of communication between the family, the school and the world outside. This is especially important where the death of a teacher or pupil is concerned, or where there has been a multiple accident or tragedy that may invite the interest of the media. No information should be given out without the consent of parents and pupil. If it is a death of a parent the child's wishes should be taken into account. If the child has been absent because of the death, the news may have leaked out by the time he returns. He may still feel he would like someone to handle the situation; in a secondary school this could be undertaken by a housemaster or head of year, who could save the child from intrusive or embarrassing questioning.

The school must see that everyone who should know is properly informed, including visiting teachers and the leaders of clubs and extra-curricular activities; if the child has to move school, information about the death and about the child's needs and problems should be passed on to the new school. This is important even if the death has occurred many years before, because if some catalyst were to occur at the next school it might prove to be a trigger for renewed grief. Knowledge about a child's physical and emotional health should travel with him throughout his school days so that an eye can be kept on his well-being.

Provide a life-raft

A teacher may be the person a child will instinctively cling to in distress, especially where the classroom relationship has always encouraged open communication and mutual trust. Opportunities for quiet talking can be found in the playground or classroom during dinner breaks, and it is very natural for a teacher to find topics that will allow a child to speak of her sorrow, problems or anxieties.

Plenty of scope should be allowed for freedom of expression through drawing, painting, modelling, play and drama and the inventing of story endings. Outline faces can be made into which different expressions – sad, lonely, surprised, happy – can be introduced and talked about.

Provide activities which are helpful to the bereaved child but do not single him or her out; for example, the whole class can bring family photos and holiday snaps or make memory books. Be mindful of anniversaries and the pain of the first Christmas without Mum or Dad.

Some children will find both reading and writing poetry therapeutic. A ten-year-old whose father had left home wrote a poem about himself which finished 'Most of all he loves his mum and dad', and he made a Valentine for the absent father. A fifteen-year-old whose father had died of a heart attack after they had had a row was plagued by remorse. He found no peace until his teacher encouraged him to write a letter to his dead father, explaining his point of view, saying sorry for his disobedience and asking for forgiveness. At this age adolescents are aware of wrongdoing and need to find healing in what they can see as an act of reparation.

Keep one step ahead

Anticipate difficult situations that may arise as a result of a bereavement in your class. One of my students had no idea what to do when an ashen-faced boy burst into her class with the words, 'I'm sorry I'm late, Miss, my sister was electrocuted this morning.' In another school a pupil's father had been killed in recent riots and the teacher thought it would be best to speak to the class before the boy returned. The teacher warned the class not to press Colin for details of his father's death, but stressed that if he wanted to talk about it he must be allowed to do so.

Watch out for unkindness

It is rare to find children being unkind to those who lose a parent, but it can happen:

> The hardest thing to face about my father's death was going back to school afterwards. I walked into assembly and someone made fun along the lines of 'It must be nice not to have a dad'.

But it is a different matter when children lose a parent to prison:

> We were all judged as guilty and ostracised. The eldest boy had a terrible time at school as did the others. Children can be

very cruel, aided and abetted by parents who don't want criminals living on their doorstep.

Watch out for signs of distress

If a teacher is to notice any abnormality in a child's appearance or behaviour, he or she must know what is normal for that child and be sensitive to the child's situation. Indications of distress may be:

- Physical: a vacant, listless or strained appearance; a constant tiredness or general ill health.

- Behavioural: very quiet and withdrawn; reluctance to participate; aggressive, angry; over-reacting or bullying.

- Educational: regression; inability to concentrate; an obsessional approach to work as a compensation. These are normal reactions; remember that weeping and grief and losing sleep make children tired and unwilling to join in. But if they become intense or out of control they will need monitoring.

- Delinquent behaviour, for example vandalism or stealing. A five-year-old Kenyan Asian girl whose father died after she had been in this country for only a year had multiple problems. She could speak little English; she had an imperfect understanding of death's finality; she had moved house and home and country, away from friends and relatives. Her confusion was obvious in her constant comments that 'the police have taken Daddy away', that 'Daddy is in the ground but soon he will be coming back' and 'my daddy doesn't like me'. This child was found with property taken from the school and from other children. Her teacher understood and found a way to help:

I feel this behaviour is her way of compensating for her loss in some way. I tell her that she must not take things that do not belong to her and I try to see that she has a painting or a piece of work that she has done to take home. I feel that the child needs to come to terms with her loss but I will keep a close eye on this tendency to take things.[4]

Books

Every classroom should contain books about death and bereavement, appropriate to the age of the students and drawn from various cultures. They should include information books, traditional fairy tales and reality-based stories. See Appendix II for details of further reading.

Overview

- The teacher is in a unique position to find ways of rebuilding a pupil's self-esteem along lines suggested earlier, by finding her skills and encouraging her to develop them.

- Give responsibilities that must be undertaken conscientiously. According to age, these may range from having the care of the classroom hamster to organising an outing for the sixth form.

- Give generous praise for achievement, courage or kindness, all those things which give a person a very positive picture of herself or himself.

- Take a personal interest in the child and keep an overview of her situation by being the one who supports the lone parent at PTA meetings.

School may be the child's only dependable environment. Teachers can nurture and restore a damaged sense of trust by being dependable people themselves, offering a firm behaviour pattern with no irrational swings to leniency or anger, being fair-minded and kindly, always there when needed.

Whole-school measures

Schools and residential homes have particular problems when large numbers of children are affected by the same event, such as the death of a teacher or the killing of children in class as in the tragedy at Dunblane. Strategies for dealing with such events should be agreed by staff and worked out beforehand. A counsellor or other professional skilled in handling traumatic grief should be consulted on how best to help the whole community.

Such procedures should be revised and kept up to date, for they cannot be brought into action without planning. Schools increasingly need to be prepared for emergencies such as road crashes, holiday accidents, national disasters and even the random killings of psychopaths, which seem now to be occurring with greater frequency.

And afterwards

One of the great benefits that the school has to offer is its continuity, giving the bereaved child a point of reference combining change with stability right through from pre-school to sixth form and perhaps beyond, where members of staff have nurtured a friendship. Many extra-curricular clubs and activities will still be available long enough for the youngster to establish a niche in the adult world, with its widening prospects.

Pastures new

Once the funeral is over and mourning has become manageable, life will begin to gain a semblance of normality. It must then be the concern of adults to provide a new start and an adequate environment. Every effort should be made to find interesting activities and new horizons that will take children out of themselves.

A pet can make a very special solace for the heart of a lonely child. A dog has an uncanny instinct for knowing when someone is sad and will either cuddle close for silent comfort or try some diverting tactics with a ball. A child can confide his deepest feelings to a dog, as to no one else, and will receive uncritical sympathetic companionship.

Young people have a fundamental need to belong to something, someone or a group other than their own family: Cubs, Scouts, Guides and other organisations (uniformed or not) draw children into a community which is independent of parents, while those with a religious affiliation, such as Crusaders, add to human companionship a spiritual dimension which can for some be a source of renewed hope and strength.

Many of these provide exactly the healing medium needed, especially for children who may have had to drop out during a parent's terminal illness:

> If, like me, you have to take the washing to the launderette on Saturday, you can't go to dancing classes on Saturday mornings, and so can't change to the second stage on Monday evenings. My social education was non-existent – I missed out on dancing lessons, tennis and so on (though fortunately I did go to Crusaders).

Holidays and outings are important:

> We tried to live as full a life as possible . . . we continued to use our caravan for holidays . . . the older members of Gill's family kept in touch, as did many of her friends.

and where holidays may be beyond the reach of some it may be possible for support groups to help:

> Rotary and other service groups have been good in organising trips for young people who have been bereaved and injured, and holiday offers for families have been made by travel agencies.

> Such shared activities have much to offer – acceptance, responsibility and challenge, boosting self-esteem.

POINTS TO REMEMBER

THE SUPPORT SYSTEM

- DO become acquainted with what support is available from the whole community and be prepared to call upon whoever seems appropriate in the circumstances. If need be, invite advice of CRUSE

- DO promote active co-operation among all helping agencies involved, whether the situation affects a single family or is a major tragedy – e.g. GPs, social workers, ministers, schools

- DO watch out for danger signals indicating an immediate need for referral to specialist help

- DO be aware of the needs of carers

- DO encourage schools, residential homes, hospitals, etc., to put in place programmes and to practice procedures ready in case of some sudden tragedy

- DO avoid taking too much on yourself, incurring burnout

SCHOOL – AN ALTERNATIVE WORLD

- DO be prepared for a bereaved child's absenteeism and disruptive or uncharacteristic behaviour on return

- DO reintegrate the bereaved child by maintaining reasonable discipline, work schedules and normal procedures

- DO make sure that everyone concerned with the bereaved child is kept informed of the situation

- DO, if need be, facilitate open communication between the surviving parent and bereaved child

8

Building defences:
preparing children to cope

Charlotte Thompson, aged seventeen, hanged herself because she thought her perfectly respectable A-level grades were not good enough to qualify her for entry to a career as a physiotherapist. She thought she was a failure.

Mark, aged fifteen, hanged himself because he could not face the bullies at his school. He felt rejected. Every week two or three British teenagers kill themselves, and the suicide rate among the young is rising. This puts a question to society. Why is it that, with all our twentieth-century advantages, our scientific knowledge and our psychological insights, we seem less able than our forebears to equip the young to cope with the crises of life?

What are the particular difficulties of bringing up children to meet the challenge of today's world?

Now you see it now . . .?

There is a sense in which everything is against the parent struggling to achieve this aim. A strong personality is a vital element in helping a child to withstand all forms of shock and adversity, including bereavement – but to nurture a stable personality a stable environment is needed. Instead, society is changing rapidly. Parents themselves are ill-equipped for their role because they too are bewildered by the pace of change.

Parents today have to meet situations which produce stresses unknown until now. It is one thing to grow up in a primitive society, learning to meet the dangers of an environment which has remained unchanged for centuries and where ancestors have devised accepted means of coping. It is something else to belong to a generation of confused parents, where the cultural scene is changing like a kaleidoscope. No wonder they have lost their confidence, and with it their authority. Both of these are important factors in bringing up children who will themselves be confident and secure.

The crumbling fabric – a disintegrating society

We no longer have the kind of structured society in which people can feel that they have a rightful place and a role to fill. At one time rural communities and large estates or urban districts offered a permanency of employment and a communal life. There was a homeliness that held the child secure. You knew what was expected of you.

A structured society gives a feeling of stability. Nowadays you are lucky to have a job for a few weeks. According to research, the increase in suicides is related to social change over the past two decades, especially in unemployment and the divorce rate,[1] and the most important factors in increasing the risk of mental health problems among the young seem to be poverty and family discord.[2]

The lost cement

The cement which held our society together for nine hundred years was a common pattern of belief. Take a walk round any churchyard and reflect on the different perspective of a hundred years ago. The epitaph 'Safe in the arms of Jesus' has merely become 'Goodbye Dad'. This is not just the concern of the Church. It means the loss of common beliefs, values, norms of behaviour.

Everything is questioned. Moral absolutes are thrown out, depriving the young of much-needed guidelines. The mother in Rosa Guy's *The Friends* spells out the problem:

It is hard, no matter how we try, to think of our children as
outside of us, with problems of their own. So naturally it's
difficult to guide them . . . Things that were right and things
that were wrong have lost their distinction. Now, what I
considered right is completely wrong, and what a short time
ago I might have considered wrong, is just the way of things.

In fact the implications are far-reaching, and shake the
foundation of our laws, which were founded on Judaeo-
Christian principles. Without the cement, society is falling
apart.

The shaky foundation – the disappearing family

Families are the place where character is formed, and the
accelerating rate at which families are breaking up means that
an increasing number of children are born into homes that do
not have the stability of a married relationship. Consequently,
an increasing number of children will be at risk if one of their
parents should die.

The primary task – looking ahead

During the last decade progress has been made in the inves-
tigation of childhood bereavement and studies now rely more
on children's own reports of their experiences and emotional
reactions. These offer valuable insights which may help
parents in their primary task – to endeavour to enable
children to cope with life whatever it may bring – and into
ways of giving children pre-emptive help before they are
overtaken by tragedy.

Teach me to die

> Teach me to die that I may dread
> The grave as little as my bed.[3]

An understanding of death – that it is inevitable, universal and natural – is an obvious first step, for children who have been educated are more likely to adapt to loss positively than those for whom it has been shrouded in mystery and taboo. It has been suggested that 'death education' should begin as young as two or three years old and programmes have been devised for pre-schoolers. As with sex education, there are those who advocate pushing these major issues on children as early as possible. I am not in favour of this. These matters are rightly the province of the home, under the aegis of parents, and should arise naturally in the ordinary course of life, in response to the initiative of children and their questions. They should not be imposed arbitrarily in deference to some well-intentioned educational or ideological theory. Children vary widely in their readiness for certain types of knowledge.

Knowledge in the making

> Searching what we know not by what we know.
>
> (Milton)

Children's learning is built on past experience, and in this respect learning about death is no different from any other learning. The child's response to the idea of death and also to bereavement will be conditioned by the way in which he has been encouraged to view his world. Night follows day, light follows darkness; autumn and winter landscapes are as captivating as the green of spring. It is an orderly universe as well as a beautiful one, and it is important that children should see death as part of that order, one of the natural laws that govern the universe. Children as young as five years old can be helped to understand and accept the idea, not as an end but as a predictable part of the continuum of the whole human experience. We are only mortal, and no one lives for ever. At the same time it is better to avoid portrayals of violence, ghosts and the occult and to keep all that is gruesome and morbid out of their store of mental imagery.

Death education is already part of the National Curriculum, so it will be a routine part of the school's function to supply appropriate teaching about death at each Key Stage and in cross-curricular activities. But talking with a child who has lost a well-loved person is a different situation. At such a time words may be meaningless and the best help may have been given long before.

It is always most important to make a point of becoming acquainted with the home beliefs, cultural background, lifestyle and interests of the child's family so as to give adequate knowledgeable support and help the child to reintegrate into the school and the wider community as soon as possible. Different cultures have different modes of expressing emotion and different rites of mourning. The Indian child may have been taught that he will be reborn, the British child will probably believe in heaven, for he will find this idea deeply rooted in the art, music and literature of our culture. You can only help people if you can stand in their shoes.

Feigned deaths

> But since that I
> Must die at last, 'tis best,
> To use myself in jest
> Thus by feigned deaths to die.
> (John Donne)

A parent's death will mean radical change in the child's life. It is helpful if they have already experienced preliminary changes which will show them that changes must come in life, but that they are not always for the worse. A child whose home base is secure can launch out on gradually lengthening absences from it with grandparents, school or camps, for instance, and by building on short and temporary partings find that he or she is able to cope without help. All such partings need to be talked through beforehand and only embarked on when the child is ready and confident. In this way she can learn creatively from all aspects of change, loss or unhappiness that she may encounter.

We should take into account the short and precious lives of pets, for though children can learn about biological death from the classroom animals, pets become part of the family and through their death we discover the price of love – that in spite of the sorrow the joy is worth it.

. . . and that says something very important in the handling of human relationships. Learning to handle the death of a pet helps children learn to cope with bereavement due to the death of a human friend or relation. It is a lesson for life never forgotten.

When Amy's rabbit was killed by a fox she wrote this letter and put it in his coffin:

Dearest Snowy,
We'll forever be friends.
You were my best friend.
You never hurt me and you were always there for me to talk to.
You were the best bunny in the world.

Competent parenting

Most parents want to help their children cope with any future hurts but are unsure how to do so. Taking the mystery away from death and giving preliminary experiences of change may help, but there are other areas where parenting is essential to the children's welfare:

i)   All children need the feeling of being held in something permanent, especially now, to counteract the flux and impermanence of social change. They need the *firm commitment and authority of responsible parents.*

ii)   All children need to acquire certain *coping skills*, one of
      the most important of which is the ability to think for
      themselves. The world of our children is virtually
      controlled by the media which portrays a much more
      exciting world than the real one. It is difficult to resist
      values presented in such compelling terms. We should
      make it plain that, though the purpose of language is to
      communicate, it may not always communicate the
      truth.

      Children who have learnt to think for themselves are
      not at the mercy of anyone who tries to manipulate
      them. They can resist the pressure of the media and the
      peer group and the 'nice' man who offers them a lift.
      The power to make decisions comes through being
      offered choices and discussing options. Young people
      in their early teens are at that exciting moment when
      they begin to make their first choices. How will they
      choose? Parents who talk through each day's events are
      helping them to cope when they themselves are no
      longer around – helping them to choose those values
      which our world needs, justice, courage, compassion,
      chastity before marriage, fidelity after. They will be
      laying the foundation of another generation of good
      parenting.

iii) In the event of a parent's death, a child's self-esteem may
      be severely undermined. We have to think of their future
      and prepare them now for what may follow in this
      unpredictable world. A secure self-image comes from
      knowing that you have a significant place in the family
      and gifts and skills that are unique to you; that your
      dreams and hopes are shared. We build such a con-
      fidence when we *affirm our love* and commitment.

iv)   It is reassuring for children if they can know that *their
      future has been thought about* and possible plans
      considered on the lines, 'If anything should happen to
      us you know you can go to Grandma, and if that is not

possible Uncle John and Auntie Jean would see that you are all right.'

v) Children watch so much television nowadays that their language development may be downgraded, but if we are hoping to communicate practicalities, let alone values, families must first *learn to communicate*. Our first strategy must be to safeguard talking time – mealtimes, bedtimes and especially when they come home from school, maybe worried about a quarrel, a low grade or something that has gone wrong. We should encourage our children to talk about their feelings, their activities and their relationships: we too need to acquire the habit of communication, to learn to walk into the area of painful feelings, and so to make it easier for our children to talk about sad things – maybe losses such as broken friendships – otherwise we may leave it too late and leave them hindered in some major loss. Children brought up in an atmosphere of mutual trust can learn to understand a parent's feelings and responses, so that without inhibiting the expression of their own grief they can share their sorrow and mourn together.

'As wheat that springeth green'

Although there is a sense in which we never 'get over' the death of someone close, eventually, almost incredibly, there will be diminutive signs of growth which can, in maturity, develop into positive benefits.

It is now thought that for children as well as adults, normal grieving continues for a year or more, but following a time of apathy, withdrawal or depression there may be a recovery, renewed energy and a different outlook on life which may have various attendant advantages. There may be a willingness to take an interest in new activities, explore new relationships and adapt to change. It may become possible to accept failure

without feeling threatened, but seeing it as a guideline to a way
forward; and perhaps most surprisingly it may mean a new
spirit of independence and a rise in self-esteem:

> I used to keep running to my mother, clinging to her. After
> she died I could face school . . . I still had my fear of school
> but I was able to cope without having my mother.

The experience of sorrow can bring a wider understanding of
both the world and one's own life, together with an ability to
enter into another person's sorrow in a way that is not possible
for those who have never grieved. Those who have suffered
themselves are best able to share, to listen and to be an
understanding companion to others in a similar plight. It is
your own experience of suffering that makes it possible to
comfort someone else. This is true too of children, who will,
from their own sorrow, try to bring the healing comfort of love
to a lone parent:

> My husband died when my daughter was aged three years
> and three months. From the beginning she accepted it well. In
> fact a few days later when I was having a weep she said,
> 'Never mind, Mummy, you'll see Daddy in heaven.'

For those who have a religious belief, finding that in the midst
of suffering they can still trust may result in a stronger faith.

Trust in God

'The child's greatest need and hardest task is to find meaning in
life,' Bruno Bettelheim has said, 'and this he finds when he
knows he is loved and accepted.' This is what makes a mother's
or father's love the most formative element in a child's life and
gives him the basic trust he needs to overcome his fears and
anxieties.

We do our best to enable children to cope with the vicissitudes
of life by nurturing this trust and by making life as safe and

predictable as we can, by assuring them that they have significance and that all is well.

But supposing there comes a time when we cannot give this assurance – when tragedy has entered their lives? Here we have to look beyond our human help and comforting to another level of trust and another source of help. At this point the beliefs of the parents will come into the picture, for parents who themselves have profound trust in the essential worth of life and the goodness of God naturally transfer those attitudes to their children.

A lonely parent can assure her children that we receive the meaning we all seek when we know we are loved and accepted by our Maker, and that the meaning he bestows on us is ours for ever. This does not mean that we will not meet sorrow and suffering and death, but it means that they do not have the last word. Most religions affirm that such an attitude is rooted in reality because God is trustworthy; and the parent who inspires this trust in a child is teaching him the nature of reality. We may not know in scientific terms how far this element of trust may contribute to the healing process, but there is good evidence that it can play a part:

> My father was killed at work by falling off a ladder when I was nearly seven years old. When my dad died, to me he had gone to be with Jesus – and that realisation made a big difference to me.

The human psyche has amazing powers of self-healing, and given the right conditions life will bloom again. As the minister in Dunblane affirmed in his sermon:

> We are not left in the darkness, and the light will return.

GUIDELINES

THINKING AHEAD: helping children to cope with loss in today's world

- DO help your child to acquire a realistic attitude towards death

- DO be aware of the pressures on children today, bearing in mind the way they are increased for bereaved children

- DO create a stable and secure home life to offset the breakdown of structures in society

- DO help children to be aware of the duplicity of the media and the possible deceptions of language

- DO encourage children to think independently and make their own decisions

- DO foster their sense of intrinsic worth by surrounding them with love

- DO give opportunities for preliminary short partings

- DO talk freely with your children and discuss contingency plans to put in place in case of necessity

- DO encourage them to join organisations and activities that offer opportunities for challenges and responsibilities that can foster their sense of belonging and self-esteem

- DO encourage an attitude of trust and hope

Notes

Chapter 1

1 Unless otherwise attributed, the extracts quoted throughout the book come from letters to the author, questionnaires and interviews with bereaved families and those who are concerned for them.
2 The Rev. David Kingdon, former principal of the Irish Baptist College, Belfast, has found this illustration helpful in comforting bereaved children.

Chapter 2

1 Donald Carson, 'Growing up a P. K.', *Evangel* Vol. 2.4 (1984).
2 From Jill Krementz, *How It Feels When a Parent Dies* (Gollancz, 1983).
3 R. S. Pynoos, 'Grief and trauma in children and adolescents', p. 2 (see Appendix II).
4 See Elisabeth Kübler-Ross, *On Children and Death* (Collier, 1993), pp. 3, 4.
5 *Woman* magazine, 26 September 1994.

Chapter 3

1 Robertson (1953). See John Bowlby, *Attachment and Loss Vol. 3* (Penguin, 1969), p. 10.
2 See Pynoos, 'Grief and trauma in children and adolescents'.
3 CRUSE leaflet.
4 Even children of pre-school age experience depression mingled with separation anxiety. It has been suggested that childhood grief has

biological effects upon the whole system, and at present we cannot tell the long-term repercussions on the still-developing brain. See Pynoos, 'Grief and trauma in children and adolescents'.
5 For the case histories of Mary and Mandy I am indebted to Christine Hawkins, Health Visitor.

Chapter 4

1 Dr Dora Black, *Bereavement Care* (1985). An international journal published three times a year by the charity CRUSE. Editors are Dr Colin Murray Parkes and Dr Dora Black.
2 John White, *The Masks of Melancholy*: A Christian Psychiatrist Looks at Depression and Suicide (IVP, 1982).
3 H. L. Witmer and R. Kotinsky, eds, *Personality in the Making: The Fact-Finding Report of the Midcentury White House Conference on Children and Youth* (Harper and Row, 1952).
4 J. H. Hendriks, D. Black and T. Kaplan, *When Father Kills Mother*, (Routledge, 1993) p. 23.
5 W. Yule and R. Williams, eds. 'Post-traumatic stress reactions in children', *Journal of Traumatic Stress*, 3 (2), 279–95.

Chapter 5

1 Sister Margaret Pennells and Susan Smith, *The Forgotten Mourners: Guidelines for Working with Bereaved Children* (Jessica Kingsley Publishers).
2 See, for instance, Hendriks, Black and Kaplan, *When Father Kills Mother*, p. 162.
3 The Rev. Nigel Copsey started a bereavement counselling service in the East End of London, called Care and Counsel, with a view to involving people trained to help children, but it did not receive adequate financial support to survive.

Chapter 6

1 Krementz, *How It Feels When a Parent Dies*.
2 CRUSE leaflet.
3 CRUSE leaflet.
4 See Jean Carr, *Another Story: Women and the Falklands War* (Hamish Hamilton, 1984).

5 Adapted from a helpful article by Keith White which first appeared in *Youthwork* (Oct.-Nov. 1992).
6 Krementz, *How It Feels When a Parent Dies*.

Chapter 7

1 I am grateful to Christine Hawkins for her account of the health visitor's role.
2 Hendriks, Black and Kaplan, *When Father Kills Mother*, pp. 22, 75, 82.
3 P. Wynnejones, *Children, Death and Bereavement* (Scripture Union, 1985).
4 Ibid.

Chapter 8

1 *Children, Teenagers and Health: The Key Data*, Open University Press, 1993, pp. 67–9.
2 *Children, Young People and Mental Distress*, Mind Information.
3 Evening hymn, 'Glory to Thee my God this night', by Bishop Thomas Ken (1637–1711).

Appendix I: Useful addresses

Association of Christian Teachers
94a London Road
St Albans
Herts AL1 1NX
Tel no: 01727 840298

CARE for the Family
53 Romney Street
London SW1P 3RF
Tel no: 0171 233 0455 and 136 Newport Road
Cardiff CF2 1DJ
Tel no: 01222 464003
Will offer practical advice and can put you in touch with
counselling.

Childline
2nd floor
Royal Mail Building
50 Studd Street
London N1 0QW
tel no: 0171 239 1000
An emergency link for children in distress.

The Children's Society
Edward Rudolf House
Margery Street
London WC1 0JL
tel no: 0171 837 4299
Runs a number of projects for children with problems in their lives.

Christian Childcare Network
10 Crescent Road
South Woodford
London E18 1JB
tel no: 0181 599 1133
Provides information about Christian childcare activity within the UK and links people seeking specialist help with suitable individuals or agencies having the necessary skills and experience.

The Compassionate Friends
53 North Street
Bristol BS3 1EN
tel no: 0117 953 9639
A voluntary organisation composed of parents who have lost children.

CRUSE
Cruse House
126 Sheen Road
Richmond
Surrey TW9 1UR
tel no: 0181 940 4818 (headquarters), 0181 332 7227 (telephone advice and counselling).
Will put you in touch with someone who can help, and runs a children's phone and letter counselling service.

Grandma's
P.O. Box 1392
London SW6 4EJ
tel no: 0171 610 3904
Provides a service for children in families affected by HIV/AIDS.

Hospice Information Service
St Christopher's Hospice
1–59 Lawrie Park Road
London SE26 6DZ
tel no: 0181 778 9252

Jewish Bereavement Counselling Service
Woburn House
Tavistock Square
London WC1H 0EZ
tel no: 0171 349 0839 (answerphone), 0171 387 4300 ext. 227
(office)

National Association for Pastoral Care in Education
Institute of Education
University of Warwick
Coventry CU4 7AL
tel no: 01203 523810

National Association of Young People's Counselling and Advisory Services (NAYPCAS)
Magazine Business House
11 Newarke Street
Leicester LE1 5SF

Rainbows
Nigel Bavidge
R. E. Centre
62 Headingley Lane
Leeds LS6 2BU
tel no: 0113 2740344
Helps children who have been bereaved through parental death, separation or divorce to work through the grieving process which follows any significant loss.

The Salvation Army
105–109 Judd Street
King's Cross
London WC1H 9TS
tel no: 0171 236 5222 and 0171 383 4230 (social services)
Provides practical help and support.

The Samaritans
Head Office: 10 The Grove
Slough SL1 1QP
tel no: 01573 532713
Offer telephone and personal support.

Schools Curriculum and Assessment Authority
Newcombe House
45 Notting Hill Gate
London W11 3JB
tel no: 0171 229 8526

Further sources of support

Barnardo's
Tanners Lane
Barkingside
Ilford
Essex IG6 1QG
tel no: 0181 550 8822

Bereavement care projects form a major part of Barnardo's work.

Resources from Barnardo's

Liz Bestic, 'Dealing with death', *Community Care*, 809, 12 Apr. 1990, pp. 16–17.

Peta Hemmings, *All About Me* (Barnardo's, 1991). A board game with cards, dice, counters and user guidelines.

Peta Hemmings, 'Communicating with children through play', in *Interventions with Bereaved Children*, pp. 9–23.
  Barnardo's inventor of the *All About Me* game explains her use of it and the principles underlying its design.

Peta Hemmings, 'Direct work techniques with bereaved children: a thematic approach', in *Bereaved Children*, pp. 23–7.

Maureen Leyland, 'Working with families before and after the death of a spouse', *Scottish Concern*, 16 Sept. 1989, pp. 37–42.

Australian resources

Bereaved Parent Support (A chapter of Compassionate Friends)
tel no: (03) 6229 4654

El Kanah Counselling Services
(various suburbs of Melbourne, Victoria)
tel no: (03) 9817 5654; (03) 9817 3530

Grief and Loss Counselling Service
tel no: (03) 6234 5245

Grief Line (helpline)
Melbourne, Victoria
tel no: (03) 9596 7799

SANDS (Stillborn and Neonatal Death Support)
Freecall 1800 265 275

The Sisters of Charity Outreach Centre
72 Fitzroy Street
Fitzroy
Melbourne
Victoria 3065
tel no: (03) 9415 1522

Bryan Meltonie and Robert Ingpen, *Beginnings and Endings with Lifetimes in Between* (Hill of Content Publishing, 86 Bourke Street, Melbourne, Victoria, Australia 3066).

Jane Warland, *Our Baby Died* (JBCE, 65 Oxford Street, Collingwood, Victoria, Australia 3066).

USA resources

Candlelighters Childhood Cancer Foundation
7910 Woodmount Avenue, Suite 460
Bethesda
MD 20814–3015, USA
tel no: (800) 366 2223

Compassionate Friends
P. O. Box 3696
Oak Brook
IL 60522–3696, USA
tel no: (708) 990 0010

Make Today Count
Mid-America Cancer Center
1235 E. Cherokee Street
Springfield
MO 65804, USA
tel no: (800) 432 2273

National Hospice Organization
1901 N. Moore Street, Suite 901
Arlington
VA 22209, USA
tel no: (800) 658 8898 (Hospice helpline)

SIDS (Sudden Infant Death Syndrome Alliance)
1314 Bedford Avenue, Suite 210
Baltimore, MD USA
tel no: (410) 653 8226; (800) 221 7437

Children

Jim and Joan Boulden, *The Last Goodbye*, I and II (Boulden, 1994). Stories, games and activities to help children work through a loss experience.

P. Giff, *Today Was a Terrible Day* (Puffin Books, 1980). Just because today is bad doesn't mean tomorrow has to be the same. Pre-school to eight.

Jill Westberg McNamara, *My Mom Is Dying: A Child's Diary* (Augsburg, 1994). Kristine turns to God for help when she knows her mother is dying. Conversations with God; childlike colour illustrations.

Janice Robert and Joy Johnson, *Thank You for Coming to Say Goodbye* (Centering, 1994). A resource for children at the time of a death, and around a funeral.

D. Sandford, *It Must Hurt a Lot: A Child's Book about Death* (Multnomah Press, 1986). A boy copes with the accidental death of his puppy.

Alan Wolfelt, *Sarah's Journey: One Child's Experience with the Death of Her Father* (Center for Loss and Life Transition, 1994).

Teenagers

Earl Grollman, *Straight Talk about Death for Teenagers* (Beacon Press, 1993).

Mark Scrivani, *When Death Walks In* (Centering, 1991). Helpful for the bereaved teenager who often grieves alone.

Alicia Sims, *Am I Still a Sister?* (Big A and Company, 1986). Sibling loss.

Helping children and teenagers grieve

Peggy Barker, *What Happened when Grandma Died?* (Concordia, 1984).

Kathleen Cassini and Jacqueline Rogers, *Death and the Classroom: A Teacher's Guide to Assist Grieving Students* (Griefwork of Cincinnati, 1989).

H. Fitzgerald, *The Grieving Child: A Parent's Guide* (Simon and Schuster, 1992).

Theresa Huntley, *Helping Children Grieve: When Someone You Love Dies* (Augsburg, 1991).

C. Jewett, *Helping Children Cope with Separation and Loss* (Harvard Common Press, 1982).

Alan Wolfelt, *Helping Children Cope with Grief: For Caregivers, Parents, Teachers, Counselors* (Accelerated Development, 1983).

Appendix II: Further reading

Adults

Background reading

D. Black, 'The Bereaved Child' in *Journal of Child Psychology and Psychiatry*, 19, 1978, pp. 287–92.

J. Bowlby, 'Pathological Mourning and Childhood Mourning' in *Journal of the American Psychoanalytic Association*, 11, 1963, pp. 500–541.

R. Lansdowne, 'The Development of the Concept of Death in Childhood' in *Bereavement Care*, 4, 2, 1985, pp. 15–17.

R. S. Pynoos, 'Grief and Trauma in Children and Adolescents' in *Bereavement Care*, 11, 1, 1992, pp. 2–10.

Some useful books for adults helping a bereaved child

Mary Bending, *Caring for Bereaved Children* (CRUSE Bereavement Care, 1993)

This brief (28 pages) book gives sensible advice on how to help a child in an immediate situation. It shows how children understand death at different ages and how they may react.

Jill Krementz, *How It Feels when a Parent Dies* (Gollancz, 1983). Children give their personal experiences of loss.

L. Pincus, *Death and the Family: The Importance of Mourning* (Faber, 1966)

Rosemary Wells, *Helping Children Cope With Grief – Facing a Death in the Family* (Sheldon Press, 1988).
Practical suggestions about how to tell a child of a parent's death and advice about dealing with their reactions.

Tessa Wilkinson, *The Death of a Child – A Book for Families* (Julia MacRae Books, 1991).
Beautifully written and illustrated. Contains a story to be read with a bereaved child about the death of a brother and extracts from C. S. Lewis, J. R. R. Tolkien, A. A. Milne and other Christian writers.

The Child and Bereavement, from the Paediatric Collection of St Christopher's Hospice.

Schools

Teachers and school libraries

Children and Bereavement, Death and Loss: What Can the School Do? National Association for Pastoral Care (1993).
All aspects of coping with the death event in school.

Atle Dyregrov, *Grief in Children – A Handbook for Adults* (Kingsley, 1991).
Aims to help adults respond appropriately to the needs of a bereaved child. Explains how children of different ages understand death.

Linda Smith, *Death: The Final Journey?* (Lion Educational, 1990).
Each chapter gives facts and personal stories followed by work assignments. Death, euthanasia, how people respond to death, and life after death. Gives Christian view of death, resurrection and Jesus. For a teenage class studying issues round death and bereavement.

William Yule and Anne Gold, *Wise Before the Event – Coping with Crisis in Schools* (Calouste Gulbenkian Foundation, 1993).
Available from Turnabout Distribution Ltd, 27 Horsell Road, London N5 1XL. Guidelines for preparing to cope with

unexpected disasters in school. Examples given from the *Herald of Free Enterprise* and Hillsborough disasters.

Resources

Penny Casdagli and Francis Gobey, *Grief, Bereavement and Change: A Quick Guide* (Daniels, 1993).
Covers the effects of grief, the place of the subject in the school curriculum, whole school policies and the National Curriculum, how to support young people in bereaved families, dealing with crisis in the school community.

Grief, Bereavement and Change: A Workshop Approach (Daniels, 1993).
Practical ideas for classroom use.

Marge Heeguard, *When Something Terrible Happens – Children Can Learn to Cope with Grief* (Woodland Press, Minneapolis, 1991).
A workbook to be filled in and illustrated by five- to twelve-year-olds working with an adult. Very helpful for enabling the free expression of feeling.

Sheila Hollins and Lester Sireling, *When Dad Died*, and *When Mum Died* (St George's Mental Health Library, 1994).
Working through loss with people who have learning disabilities or with children.

Linda Machin, *Working With Young People in Loss Situations: A Work Pack* (Longman, 1993).
Useful manual which explores the effects of grief upon young people and provides a resource for carers and professionals supporting and counselling children. Part 1 offers suggestions and guidance for using visual material, Part 2 provides an insight into the experience of loss in childhood, and Part 3 contains picture resources.

Anthea Millar and Angela Cameron, *Active Listening: A Counselling Skills Approach* (Daniels, 1994).

Barbara Ward and associates, *Good Grief: Exploring Feelings, Loss and Death with Under-11s*; and *Good Grief: Exploring Feelings, Loss and Death with Over-11s* (both Kingsley, 1993).

Together these make an excellent resource for schools. *Under-11s* provides a framework for exploring feelings and issues around loss and death for children of different abilities.

Over-11s contains activities with photocopiable worksheets, articles, booklists and addresses.

Agnes Whitaker, ed., *All in the End is Harvest: An Anthology for Those who Grieve* (Darton, Longman and Todd in association with CRUSE, 1994).

Could be used for creative writing or art work, or for pupils composing a service.

Children

Books may provide comforting opportunities for small children to sit on someone's lap and be 'specialled'. They make it easy for a bereaved child to talk freely about what has happened, to ask questions, to recall memories – and remembering help;.

Pre-school and nursery

John Burningham, *Granpa*: (Jonathan Cape, 1994). A little girl and her grandfather enjoy doing things together. At the end his chair is empty. For adult and child to talk about what is happening.

Sheila Lamont, *Ewen's Little Brother* (Victoria Publications, 1988). Ewen and his little brother love playing together. The brother becomes ill and dies. Ewen goes to the funeral. He knows his brother is in heaven and does not need his body any more. Colourful picture book.

Doris Stickney, *Water Bugs and Dragonflies*, (Mowbray, 1982). A parable from nature making clear the finality of death. Contains advice for parents on what to say to children, prayers for a child and parents and some Bible quotes. Could be used for a terminally ill child, for loss of sibling, for a very young or older primary-age child and for Christian or non-Christian family.

7–10 years

Susan Varley, *Badger's Parting Gifts* (Picture Lions, 1994). Old
   Badger knows he will die soon but he is not afraid. Dying is
   described as running easily down a long tunnel. His friends
   are sad but they each have a special memory which is his
   parting gift for them to treasure.

It is easier to talk about personal concerns when they are the
sorrows, hopes and fears portrayed in a story. Many children
may wonder why their prayers for someone they love to get well
seem to be unheard. The following books approach this difficult
question from a Christian perspective:

Anthea Dove, *When My Brother Died* (Catholic Truth Society,
   1987).
Sue Holden, *My Daddy Died and It's All God's Fault* (Word,
   1991).
Carolyn Nystrom, *Emma Says Goodbye* (Lion Publications,
   1994).
Patricia St John, *The Tanglewoods Secret* (Scripture Union,
   1948).

In myths and legends death is often pictured as beautiful and not
to be feared, and many traditional fairy tales portray love as
stronger than death, though some very beautiful ones are more
suitable for children who have become familiar with the
language of poetry than for the very young:

Briar Rose, Sleeping Beauty, Beauty and the Beast
Hans Andersen, *The Little Match Girl*
Charles Kingsley, *The Water Babies*
Andrew Lang's Fairy Books (e.g. 'The Water of Life' in the *Pink
   Fairy Book*)
George Macdonald, *At the Back of the North Wind*
Oscar Wilde, *The Selfish Giant*

Stories of saints and martyrs and of heroic death tell children that there are some things that are more important than life itself and are worth dying for:

John Bunyan, *Pilgrim's Progress*
Roger Lancelyn Green, *King Arthur and His Knights of the Round Table*
Roger Lancelyn Green, *Robin Hood*
C. S. Lewis, *The Last Battle* (and the entire Narnia cycle)
Rosemary Sutcliff, *The Shield Ring*

Young teenagers

Children who experience the loss of someone close usually go through a series of psychological and emotional states involving a painful tangle of feelings. It may help them to understand those feelings, and to find relief in realising that other people too have had similar distress, if they can explore the common sorrow, anger, guilt and pain in the responses of fictional characters:

Judy Blume, *Tiger Eyes*
M. Craven, *I Heard the Owl Call My Name*
Rosa Guy, *The Friends*
Linda Hoy, *Your Friend, Rebecca*
Elizabeth Laird, *Red Sky in the Morning*
K. Paterson, *Bridge to Terabithia*
Jean Ure, *One Green Leaf*
Paul and Bonnie Zindel, *A Star for the Latecomer*

Appendix III:
Further examples of real situations and practical solutions

Caring for children in a refugee camp during war conditions by May Moore

Children who are separated from their parents in wars and lose contact with them live in the midst of a protracted bereavement. They are unable to complete the work of mourning, fearing all the time that their parents are dead, but living in hope that one day they may be reunited.

Creative activities can offer a medium of healing for such children, giving them a distraction from their immediate predicament, an emotional release and a certain sense of achievement.

In 1974 the mainland Turks invaded Cyprus. This resulted in the island being divided into two areas: the Turkish Cypriots in the north and the Greek Cypriots in the south of the island. Soon after the war, refugee camps were set up for the thousands of Greek Cypriots who had fled from the northern area and it was in one of these camps that Peter and I lived and worked in 1974–75.

I started English and handicraft classes on the camp for children between the ages of about four and twelve years old to keep them occupied for a few hours a day and these observations are the result of my close contact with many of them. They should be seen in the context of my having lived in Cyprus for only two years at the time, with a very limited understanding of the language. However, after having lived on the island for seventeen years I still feel that my perceptions of those years were correct.

In general children in Cyprus are spoilt, particularly boys and especially if they are the only son; but they are not shielded from traumatic incidents (e.g. fierce arguments between parents or other adults) or death (e.g. slaughtering of animals, attending funerals). Emotions and feelings are very much up-front and children learn from adults to laugh aloud if happy and to cry openly when tragedy strikes. In this framework, when they fled their towns and villages with their families during the war they had to cope with two dramatic changes in their lives: being uprooted suddenly from their homes, in most cases without any possessions save the clothes they were wearing; and, often, the disappearance of their father or older brother(s).

For months after the invasion everyone was convinced that they would be returning to their homes before too long. Only a handful did not hold this belief. Those children who found out quite soon that their father or brother had been killed went through the normal period of mourning that was expected. Because of strong family ties, including the extended family, and the support (both emotional and material) they received from each other, and because feelings were not bottled up, the children settled into their daily lives quite quickly, but of course continued to miss their father or brother.

However, the media and, for school-age children, the propaganda taught to them at school, together with talk on the camp, kept the war and its tragic consequences in the forefront of their minds so that they had no opportunity to forget what had happened to their loved ones. Many of them became aggressive and warlike in their play, but so did children who had not lost a member of their family.

In my classes I would ask the children to make specific things with materials provided (e.g. necklaces, purses) but with crayons and coloured strips of paper and material I would let them create what they wanted. The boys were rarely interested in making 'jewellery' or sewing, although some of them produced things they were proud of. All of them, however, boys and girls, through the whole age range, would draw and colour or create a collage of either a complete war scene or at least one bomb being dropped on their house or tent.

The aura around families who did not know whether their missing menfolk were alive or dead was distinct: it was as if they were in a state of limbo and children reflected this state of mind. Some of the children were a little more subdued than their peers, others displayed difficult behaviour, began stuttering or had unusual fears, etc. Underlying the daily life of these families and children was a state of anxiety, waiting and waiting to hear if their father or brother was dead, or a prisoner of war, or on the point of being released.

Within my classes the behaviour of these children was no different to the others. Very seldom did I have any problems with discipline and it did pass my mind that the room they were in, with a foreigner who could not verbally communicate with them very well, might be an oasis for them and a refuge from the emotional stresses and strains of adult distress and war propaganda they were unremittingly exposed to.

Experiences of prisoners' wives and their families – hardship, distress and improvement contributed by members of Prison Fellowship

The loss of a father to imprisonment is a painful form of bereavement which is neither understood nor regarded with sympathy by the public at large. Children of prisoners become included in a general aura of condemnation, and are often mocked and tormented at school. Wives are torn between the desire to visit their husband, with all the travelling and financial problems involved, and the need to care for the children. In many prisons no provision is made for young children visiting.

However, in some detention centres the influence of Chaplains and Probation Officers is bringing about a growth of understanding of the plight of prisoners' families and conditions have improved for children visiting their fathers.

Throughout this account the situation has been considered as applying only to fathers, because of the high proportion of fathers in prison, but in fact it is even more difficult for mothers in prison to make arrangements for their families.

January 13th in 1977 was just a normal day until my husband failed to come home at 1.00 p.m. from his job as a postman. I felt uneasy – something was wrong. When I saw him get out of a car between two men my heart sank and a feeling of dread came over me. His head was held down, his eyes on the pavement. After a very short conversation he told me that he had been arrested and that he had to go to the police station.

When he had gone I just cried and cried. I asked a neighbour if she would pick the children up from school as I had to visit an aunt who lived six miles away.

When my husband went to prison I was unable to attend court because I had to be there for the children. His case was heard at 2.00 p.m. and I had no one to mind them when they came out of school.

It had not been a good marriage. Things had been very difficult, and I had suffered abuse. As he was taken to prison and he wasn't going to be home for eighteen months, I put in for a divorce. We were *very* poor at that time and I remember I could not afford to buy the twelve-year-old a pair of shoes. She had to wear mine but they were far from new. She never made a fuss – they were very old-fashioned and the children at school were not nice to her.

My husband was first sent to Wormwood Scrubs and then, a few weeks later, to a prison in Sussex. The car needed new valves and I had very little cash so we never visited him. No one came to tell us if there was any help to be had. No Probation Officer came, no Social Services. I knew nothing about any help I could have had or where to go – if there was anywhere.

Our family was like an island. We drew closer to one another during this time.

When I look back I wish I had talked more to the children to help them understand, and encouraged them to express their feelings. I realise now how they were suffering as much pain as I was. Their young lives were turned upside down too, and they had lost their father suddenly and without warning.

From *When Father Kills Mother* by Hendriks, Black and Kaplan (Routledge).

Each year, in England and Wales alone, 100,000 children are estimated to experience the imprisonment of their fathers. More than 3,000 a year are likely to suffer the imprisonment of their mothers . . . however, when mothers go to prison children face far more disruption.

There is surprisingly little research on psychiatric disorders or school difficulties among the children of prisoners. The most relevant information comes from the study of children who have suffered the break-up of their families through divorce. Indeed many children suffer from repeated spells of parental imprisonment and more than one divorce as well. Psychiatric disorder and delinquency are common sequels to such adversities.

Examples from schools where a bereavement has occurred and where procedures are in place for any future such contingency

Within the last few years national tragedies have vividly illustrated the fact that these can occur anywhere, any time. It is important for institutions such as schools, where children spend so much of their time, to be aware of children's needs in such situations and to think ahead how best to cope with them.

A non-denominational primary school

We knew that the member of staff would not return to school and that she was going to die very shortly. When this information came, I explained to the children in assembly. I told them she was very ill and the doctors and nurses were doing everything they possibly could. We said prayers for her every day.

When the news arrived that she had died (and it was very quick) each member of staff told their class and they spent a short time talking about death and their memories of the teacher. The children responded very positively. Some children wrote poems and some drew pictures. These were sent to her husband.

On the day of the funeral we had a service for the children and staff who didn't attend the funeral. There was media interest, but I didn't follow it up because I could not speak to her husband and felt it was for him to decide if he wished for a newspaper article.

We have set up a memorial fund and in the autumn term we will have a service for parents and children and her husband – a celebration of her life as a teacher at our school. Death is covered in RE lessons, but at present this is not set in a policy or scheme of work.

A denominational secondary school

Our pastoral system is organised into Year Teams comprising Form Tutors and Attached Teachers led by Heads of Year under the direction of members of the Senior Management Team. In addition, we have a Pastoral Assistant, a direct employee of the school, who combines the work of an Educational Welfare Officer with that of School Counsellor and Home School Liaison Officer. We have two Heads of

Year engaged in the school's attendance project (attendance is currently 92.5 per cent). The whole Pastoral Team meets once a week to discuss attendance issues and causes of absence. Our work with bereaved pupils derives from these meetings as any domestic difficulties affecting attendance or progress will be discussed at them. The Pastoral Assistant and Head of Year will be available to the bereaved pupil for counselling for as long and as often as it is needed. It is often requested by the families of the bereaved, although it is our published policy that the pupil may approach any member of staff with whom he or she feels comfortable, and that person will make him or herself available. In addition, we are helped by our school Chaplain and the priests of our Deanery.

When one of our colleagues died in tragic circumstances five years ago, staff members were helped very much by three priests in the Deanery. In the case of deaths of pupils or teachers, the bereavement will begin at the funeral. We would seek for the members of the school community to be as involved as the family would wish or allow. Our experience is that families want the school to be involved and welcome as much participation as possible.

In addition, support will be given to classmates through the Pastoral and Social Education programme (the Head of PSE attends the Pastoral Meetings, as does the Head of Theology), and they will be advised about how to help the bereaved pupil. The PSE programme deals with the topic in Years Seven, Eight and Ten. Modules last for about three weeks. The younger children will be introduced to the topic through such things as deaths in soap operas. The older children cover the subject as part of the module dealing with family breakdown, which will itself require a grieving process. While the RE programme does not deal directly with the topic, it would be a natural and obvious place for pupils and teachers to raise the matter.